Medical Insurance Schemes for the Poor

Medical Insurance Schemes for the Poor

WHO BENEFITS?

Editor

RAMA V. BARU

ACADEMIC FOUNDATION
NEW DELHI

www.academicfoundation.org

First published in 2015
by

ACADEMIC FOUNDATION
4772-73 / 23 Bharat Ram Road, (23 Ansari Road),
Darya Ganj, New Delhi - 110 002 (India).
Phones : 23245001 / 02 / 03 / 04.
Fax : +91-11-23245005.
E-mail : books@academicfoundation.com
www.academicfoundation.org
www.academicfoundation.com

Cataloging in Publication Data--DK
Courtesy: D.K. Agencies (P) Ltd. <docinfo@dkagencies.com>

Medical insurance schemes for the poor : who benefits? /
editor, Rama V. Baru.
pages cm
Contributed articles.
ISBN 9789332701908

1. Health insurance--India. 2. Poor--Medical care--Government policy--India. I. Baru, Rama V., 1959-, editor.

DDC 368.38200954 23

Typeset by Italics India, New Delhi.

Printed and bound by The Book Mint, New Delhi.
www.thebookmint.in

CONTENTS

LIST OF TABLES AND FIGURES

Tables

Figures

About the Editor/Contributors

Editor:

Rama V. Baru, Professor, Centre of Social Medicine and Community Health, Jawaharlal Nehru University, New Delhi.

Contributors:

Archana Diwate, Research Scholar, Centre of Social Medicine and Community Health, Jawaharlal Nehru University, New Delhi.

S. Garg, Senior Programme Coordinator, State Health Resource Centre, Raipur, Chhattisgarh.

S. Haripriya, Research Scholar, Department of Sociology, Delhi School of Economics, University of Delhi, Delhi.

C.J. Jisha, Research Scholar, Centre of Social Medicine and Community Health, Jawaharlal Nehru University, New Delhi.

K. Kanungo, Research Fellow, Public Health Foundation of India (PHFI), Delhi NCR.

H. Khan, Programme Associate (Maternal Health Division), State Health Resource Centre, Raipur, Chhattisgarh.

T. Mishra, Project Coordinator, Narotam Sekhsaria Foundation, Mumbai, Maharashtra.

Ankita Mukherjee, Research Scholar, Centre of Social Medicine and Community Health, Jawaharlal Nehru University, New Delhi.

S. Nandi, State Convener, Public Health Resource Network (PHRN), Raipur, Chhattisgarh.

M. Nundy, Associate Fellow, Institute of Chinese Studies, New Delhi.

N. Purendra Prasad, Professor, Department of Sociology, School of Social Sciences, University of Hyderabad, Hyderabad.

V. Prasad, National Convener, Public Health Resource Network (PHRN), New Delhi.

Kaushik Sakia, Research Scholar, Centre of Social Medicine and Community Health, Jawaharlal Nehru University, New Delhi.

1

RAMA V. BARU

Inequities in Access to Medical Care

Is Insurance the Answer?

During the last two decades, the challenge to health services has been to address growing regional and socio-economic inequalities in developing and developed countries. The evidence has raised a host of ethical and moral dilemmas around the exclusion of those who need health care the most. The reason for the exclusion was attributed to introduction of the new public management in health services that privileged the market and restructured the role of the state. These ideas found their way into the content and design of health sector reforms both globally and nationally. Multilateral agencies like the World Bank played a proactive role in furthering this agenda by making it a part of the Structural Adjustment Programme with inclusion of the health sector for lending. The *World Development Report* entitled "Investing in Health" that provided a detailed blueprint of the design of health service system was extremely influential in developing and developed countries. This report was influential in setting the discourse on how to restructure health services among bilateral organisations, international NGOs (non-governmental organisations), academia, scientific and professional bodies. An epistemic community of these various actors who shared the ideological basis of the need and scope for these reforms dominated the debate during the latter part of the 20th century. The voice of the sceptics and critics went unheard or dismissed during this period.

As the health sector reform agenda unfolded and far reaching structural changes were instituted, the effects were showing some worrying trends. The data from several African countries who had introduced measures for commercialisation of the health services showed that the regional and social inequalities in access had widened. In addition, the poor were being excluded due to the inability to pay and the levels of out-of-pocket expenditures were on the rise. A similar picture was beginning to emerge from some Latin American and South Asian countries as well. This body of evidence strengthened the concerns raised by the sceptics and the critics of health sector reform. This resulted in a vibrant debate in several global and national forums during this period.

The importance of medical insurance schemes for the poor gained currency in the aftermath of the health sector reforms of the 1980s and 1990s. These reforms that were guided by ideas of privatisation and commercialisation of health services led to restructuring the role of the state and enlarging spaces for market forces within the health service systems. The euphoria of these reform measures were short lived in view of the growing evidence of rising inequalities in access to services, high out-of-pocket expenditures and the exclusion of those who required care the most. Several critics of the reform process argued that these inequalities in access had to be addressed through policies that would ensure inclusion of the poor and other vulnerable sections of the population. Financing mechanisms like medical insurance schemes were suggested as a viable option to improve access to the poor. There were many models of insurance schemes that had been initiated by NGOs in Africa and Asia during the 1980s. Some of these were initiated with the support of donor agencies, while others partnered with public and private insurance companies. These were normally small-scale initiatives and confined to communities where the NGOs were functioning. When the problem of rising costs and inequalities became a serious concern for health service systems globally, the idea of targeted medical insurance schemes became part of policy discourse. These discourses were initiated at the global and national levels.

The debate on the nature, scope and consequences of health sector reform was actively debated in India. There was an ideological divide between those who defended these reforms and those who were critical of it. For those who defended the reforms, markets were the answer to state failure in health services. The critics, on the other hand, argued that market failures in health services were well known and therefore the state cannot abdicate its responsibility. They emphasised the need to correct structural anomalies of public services. Several scholars analysed the National Sample Survey (NSS) data to point out that between the late 1980s and mid-1990s, there was a considerable shift in utilisation patterns from the public to the private sector for outpatient and inpatient services.

The reason for these shifts were attributed to several reform initiatives like introduction of user charges in public hospitals, lack of adequate government investment, and the splitting of preventive and curative services. In addition, the expansion of private sector for tertiary care and diagnostic facilities were responsible for the shift. The analysis showed the inequalities in access had widened and the proportion of those who did not access medical care due to their inability to pay had increased. The government recognised these growing inequalities and rising out-of-pocket expenditures on medical care as a serious concern that was highlighted in the Tenth and Eleventh Plan documents of the Planning Commission. Several scholars demonstrated the negative consequences of rising out-of-pocket expenditures on poverty levels (Selvaraj and Karan, 2009). The high out-of-pocket expenditure was due to higher levels of utilisation of the private sector. It was estimated that 97 per cent of total private and 80 per cent of total health expenditure was out-of-pocket, which put an enormous burden on the poor. It is often assumed that the burden of expenditure on medical care is high only for inpatient services but this is actually not the case. Baru *et al.* (2010) show that the burden is high for both outpatient and inpatient services with the poor and lower income quintiles being the worst affected. What one observes is a gradient in the burden of expenditure across income quintiles for outpatient and inpatient care in rural and urban areas (see Figures 1.1 and 1.2). While the poorest quintile bears the highest burden, it is quite high for 7 out of the 12 remaining quintiles in rural areas. In the case of urban areas, the poor and middle quintiles bear a fairly high burden.

Figure 1.1

Burden of Direct Health Expenditure on the Household for Outpatient and Inpatient Treatment in Rural Areas, 2004

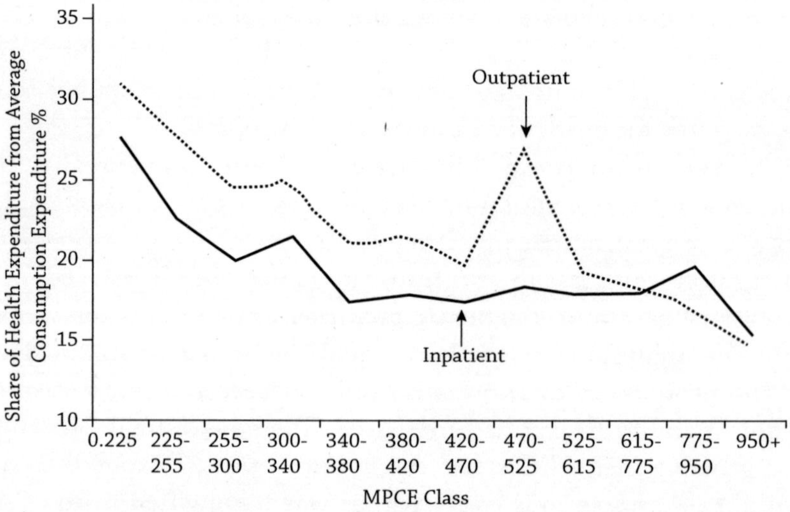

Source: NSSO, 2006.

Figure 1.2

Burden of Direct Health Expenditure on the Household for Outpatient and Inpatient Treatment in Urban Areas, 2004

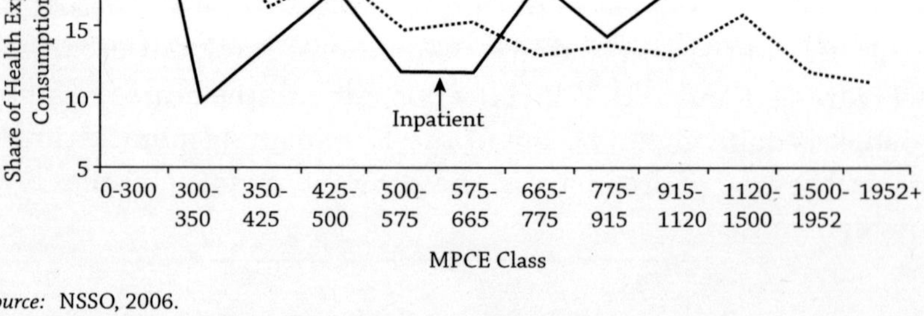

Source: NSSO, 2006.

The policy response to these trends was focused on financing and provisioning. Targeted insurance schemes for inpatient care was seen as a viable strategy to address both cost and access concerns. In rural areas, the National Rural Health Mission (NRHM) was launched in 2005 to revitalise the health services in selected districts and states with central funding. The major targeted insurance schemes include the Rajiv Arogyasri from Andhra Pradesh and the Rashtriya Swasthya Bima Yojana (RSBY) which is centrally sponsored.

The proposed volume is a collection of essays that examine the conceptual underpinnings and design of insurance schemes for the poor. Based on empirical studies, it also highlights the experience of beneficiaries who are covered by three major types of insurance schemes that are initiated by an NGO, state and central governments.

The introduction to the volume provides an overview of the growing importance of insurance schemes in addressing the growing inequities in access to health services and rising out-of-pocket expenditures for the poor and middle classes. An important reason for these inequities in access was due to commercialisation of health services since the 1980s which accelerated during the subsequent decades. It further argues that the design of NGO and state-led models were informed by a partnership between the public and private sectors.

The second chapter by Kaushik Saikia provides a conceptual and historical overview of the idea of community-based health insurance schemes that were first implemented in Africa in order to improve access for the poor who were unable to pay for services. Subsequently, several NGOs across the developing world innovated on the community-based health insurance model as a means to improve access to poorer sections of the population. This chapter also reviews these schemes and highlights the strengths and weaknesses of such an approach.

The third chapter by Archana Diwate is a qualitative study of a medical insurance scheme initiated by the union of rag pickers in Pune municipality. It describes the design, scope and depth of the scheme. It highlights the experiences of workers in accessing the scheme.

The fourth chapter by N. Purendra Prasad presents the case of Rajiv Gandhi Arogyashri, a state-led insurance programme for hospitalisation in Andhra Pradesh. This scheme played an important model for several other states to emulate. The author of the study contextualises the insurance scheme in the context of rampant commercialisation and how it privileges the interests of corporate and private hospitals in the state. The significance of this scheme is that it served as a model for other states to adapt for secondary and tertiary medical care. These schemes have led to cost inflation and many of these schemes proved to be financially unsustainable in the long run.

The fifth chapter by Ankita Mukherjee describes the history and design of the RSBY, a public insurance scheme for the poor, initiated by the Ministry of Labour, Government of India (GoI). This centrally sponsored scheme (CSS) has been adapted by different state governments to improve access to curative services to those below the poverty line.

The sixth chapter by Nandi *et al.* examines the socio-political context of RSBY and undertakes a case study of Durg, Chhattisgarh. They show the limitations of the scheme and also how it privileges the private sector.

The seventh chapter by C.J. Jisha is a case study of the modified RSBY that was renamed as Comprehensive Health Insurance Scheme to include households below and above poverty line in Kerala. The author examines the design, actors and implementation of the scheme. They highlight the conflicts and contradictions that arise from the interaction between the public insurance scheme with a mixed economy in provisioning. These studies also highlight the barriers to the utilisation of the scheme from the perspective of beneficiaries.

In summary, the strength of this book is that it provides empirical insight from different contexts in the working of medical insurance schemes for the poor in India. It raises questions regarding the limitation of targeted medical insurance schemes for the poor in a society where the large, differentiated middle class is also vulnerable when it comes to accessing medical care. Medical insurance schemes focus on curative services—a comprehensive approach that includes preventive, promotive, curative and rehabilitative care. In a context where there is rampant commercialisation of health services, public insurance schemes become subsidies for the private sector. Third party agencies who implement the insurance schemes, private hospitals that are empanelled by these schemes stand to gain. A review of several state insurance schemes shows that the proportion of private hospitals that are empanelled is higher than the public hospitals (La Forgia and Nagpal, 2012). There is also evidence of corruption seeping into the process of selection of Third Party Administrators (TPAs) and empanelling of private hospitals in several states.

The evidence from the US regarding targeted public insurance scheme in a market-dominated model of health services shows that the challenges to equity remain largely unchanged. The public subsidies in the form of medical benefits in the name of the poor has benefited the 'for profit' sector that includes providers and third party actors. Clearly, there is a strong empirical evidence from both India and abroad that points to the limits of medical insurance to address inequities.

References

Baru, R., A. Acharya, S. Acharya, A.K. Shivakumar and K. Nagaraj (2010). "Inequities in Access to Health Services in India: Caste, Class and Region", *Economic and Political Weekly* XLV(38): 49-58. 18 September.

Berman, P., R. Ahuja and L. Bhandari (2010). "The Impoverishment Effect of Health Care Payments in India: New Methodology and Findings", *Economic and Political Weekly* 45(16): 65-71

La Forgia, G. and S. Nagpal (2012). *Government-Sponsored Health Insurance in India : Are you Covered?* Washington D.C.: The World Bank.

NSSO (2006). "Morbidity, Health Care and the Condition of the Aged", *National Sample Survey 60th Round* (January-June 2004). Report No507. New Delhi: Ministry of Statistics and Programme Implementation, Government of India.

Selvaraj, S. and A. Karan (2009). "Out-of Pocket Health Expenditure and Impoverishment in India: What Causes Households to Incur Catastrophic Payments?" Paper presented at the 7th *World Congress on Health Economics* held at Beijing. July 12-15.

2

KAUSHIK SAIKIA

Socio-economic Determinants of Targeted Medical Insurance for the Poor

An Overview

Conceptualising the term 'health' is complex and difficult. The term has been defined from many perspectives. Initially the term health had a very organic definition, which was limited to the body, its organs, bodily functions and abilities. In 1946, the World Health Organization (WHO) tried to define health in a holistic way by adopting the definition as: "A state of complete physical, mental and social wellbeing and not merely the absence of disease or infirmity."[1] In 1984, the WHO extended the definition to include: "The extent to which an individual or a group is able to realise aspirations and satisfy needs, and to change or cope with the environment; health is a resource for everyday life, not the objective of living; it is a positive concept, emphasising social and personal resources as well as physical capabilities" (Wanke *et al.*, 1995) to the earlier definition of health. The idea of including social relationships, individual aspirations and the political aspect of life to the existing definition has helped for a holistic perspective of health. The concept of health is thus influenced by the interplay of macro, meso and micro level socio-economic, political determinants of health (Wanke *et al.*, 1995).

As argued by health economists, the health financing system plays a key role in reducing mortality and morbidity among population. Health financing system plays a big role in making funding available, as well as to set the right financial incentives for providers to ensure that all individuals have access to effective public health and personal

1. Preamble to the Constitution of WHO, 1946, as available on *http://www.who.int/about/definition/en/print.html* as accessed on 18 December 2009.

health care. This means reducing or eliminating the possibility that an individual will be unable to pay for care, or will be impoverished as a result of trying to do so (WHO, 2000; 2007).

There are inherent problems in this approach because health financing strategies that are adopted generally are influenced by the national and international economic politics and lobbying, and not always by the interest of people.

Impact of Change in Global Economic Paradigm on Health Policies of Developing Countries

A closer examination of the historical development of targeted health insurance provides an insight into the paradigm shift in economic thought and principles at the global and national level. Tritter *et al.* (2010) argue that there are three distinct phases of economic and health sector reform in the developed world, largely influenced by the prevalent economic schools of thought like Vilfredo Pareto, Keynes and significant others.

The health care financing mechanism in the last three decades has seen two major shifts in its paradigm. The first major reform in health financing policies at global level came after the adoption of Alma Ata declaration in 1978 and later in the late 1970s with the Structural Adjustment Programme (SAP).

Globally, majority of the low and middle income countries realised that Primary Health Care (PHC) approach was the only viable way to address national health issues and widen the public health delivery services across countries. The PHC was not only seen as a desirable way but reiterated the importance of the government's political commitment for inclusive development. The realignment of the national health financing policies started showing gaps in the resource required and available to implement the PHC strategy. Many sceptics and critics used the lack of financial resources to prevent the implementation of PHC approach. During this period, De Ferranti had calculated that there was a global resource gap of $50 billion in implementing PHC (Lee and Goodman, 2002). During the same period, the global economic recession of the late 1970s put additional financial burden on the low and middle income countries forcing them to adopt SAP in order to tide over their fiscal crisis. The World Bank in partnership with United Nations Children's Fund (UNICEF) supported academic research that proposed a shift from the principles of the PHC concept that emphasised universality, equity and comprehensiveness to reforming health systems on the ideas of economic efficiency and effectiveness. Therefore, the emphasis was on implementing measures that would improve effectiveness in the national health financing paradigms (Lee and Goodman, 2002).

The new global economic paradigm focused on three major parameters while designing the health care service delivery mechanism. These included (Akin *et al.*, 1987):

- Promoting spending on cost-effective health activities.
- Reducing internal inefficiency of health programmes.
- Effective and equitable distribution of the benefit of the health services.

The World Bank also suggested certain mechanisms to increase efficiency of health financing in developing countries, which includes but are not limited to (Akin *et al.*, 1987):

- Charge users of the public/government health facilities.
- Provide insurance or other risk coverage to the low income households.
- Decentralise government health services.

Through these initiatives, the World Bank paved the way for restructuring publicly funded health financing system to a co-payment and targeted insurance based model of health financing. As part of these initiatives, the global experiments with the targeted insurance started around mid-1980s. The first one was the UNICEF-supported Bamako Initiative and the revolving Drug Fund in Western Africa. Globally, US Agency for International Development (USAID), Department for International Development (DFID), World Bank and some UN agencies started commissioning research and experiments with health insurance both in public health services and at community-based level to show that insurance can be the way forward to meet the resource gap so as to implement selective PHC models and ensure better health service delivery (Lee and Goodman, 2002). At the same time, the shift in polices towards financing reforms showed emergence of neo-liberal approaches to social policy, resulting in the promotion of structural adjustment policies that imposed restrictions on public sector health spending in many countries. This was the second wave of shift in paradigm in health care financing at the global level (Brugha and Zwi, 2002).

Zwi and Mills (1995) observe that during this period, WHO failed to provide leadership for international health policy resulting in the World Bank gaining greater influence in shaping national policies for health systems and disease control programmes. In 1987, the Bank officially recommended that governments:

> Encourage the management sector (including non-profit groups, private physicians, pharmacists and other health practitioners) to provide health services for which consumers are willing to pay and also provide alternative financing mechanism to protect the interest of the people who cannot afford to pay.

The national health objective was to be met by selection of an effective financing system which combined effective service delivery, generated revenues for providers, met the national health priorities and also kept in mind the national budgetary constraints and inflationary pressure of public spending in national economy (Haddad *et al.*, 2008; Bloom, 2001). Most low and middle income countries struggled to achieve a rational balance between the promises made by the national policies to provide universal health security and the actual delivery of promises. The struggle was about the social inclusion of vulnerable populations and economic feasibility of the method to achieve it (Drouin, 2007).

The rising cost of medical care became the deciding factor to be able to access treatment, choice of the type of treatment and being able to afford treatment. These factors clearly had implications for health equity. The stagnation of public spending on health resulted in the reduced role for public responsibility as well as in the emergence of the private sector that was seen to provide services that were more efficient and of better quality (Bonilla-Chachin *et al.*, 2003; Tuohy *et al.*, 2004).

The health sector reform with its reliance on the market was supposed to provide efficient, effective and affordable health care services. In reality, the rise of market resulted in growing inequalities in access to services in the developed and developing countries. There were inequalities in the distribution of services with the private health care often concentrating in urban areas and in the wealthier regions in rural areas. This led to variations in the availability of services and excluded those who needed care the most. With limited state health coverage and unaffordable private health care, people from the low and middle income group suffered the most. The growth of the private sector privileged curative over preventive thus undermining an integrated and comprehensive health services delivery. The national health policies became increasingly fragmented and vertical, with the increasing emphasis on selected disease-based interventions and new entities for various health issues. These trends were in contrast to the stated aims of integrating health policy making with the broader development agenda or with comprehensive health sector planning. The poor and the socially marginalised paid the price for the global reforms (Ollila, 2005).

Due to the failure on the part of both public and market to provide health care services, alternative health financing methods were experimented with to protect the interest of the poor and ensure health services accessibility to a certain level. A key component of this initiative was identifying innovative, alternative health care demand side financing that would be matched with a public-private mix in provisioning. The demand side financing initiatives ranged from donor-driven initiatives to large-scale government-subsidised efforts towards for-profit businesses, user charges and promoting various kinds of health insurance.

In this changing global economic paradigm, community-based health insurance (CBHI) and similar targeted health insurance schemes were seen as an alternative to provide localised comprehensive health security to people. A broad working definition of CBHI is: "Any scheme managed and operated by an organisation, other than a government or private for-profit company, that provides risk pooling to cover all or part of the costs of health care services" (Bennett, 2004). This definition has three major components i.e., community initiative for risk pooling, voluntary membership to the schemes and prepayment for health care associated cost. The CBHI

(Ahuja, 2004) generally developed around some common entities such as:

- Geographical entity like village, block and local self-governance area.
- Professional entity like trade union and informal workers union.
- Service provider like hospital, bank or credit society or a community-based/ NGOs (non-governmental organisations).

CBHI and its Derivatives

The most prominent arguments for the implementation of CBHI schemes are that failure of the public health service system is the root cause of inequity in health, and CBHI was viewed as a step to build the prepayment mechanism and prepare population for private insurance scheme, large or small scale. Bennett (2004) and Devadasan *et al.* (2004) had evolved a typology based on the different models of CBHI in their respective research.

The Case for Localised Targeted Health Insurance

Most of the developing and underdeveloped countries were newly independent countries from British, French and Dutch colonial rule. One of the general characteristics of these countries was that they were resource poor and they had low per capita income. Due to the less availability of capital for public spending and stagnation of the public spending in health, private and external spending (including loans, grants and services in kind) constituted a higher share in the total spending in health.

One of the major problems for the governments in developing and underdeveloped countries was to ensure the access to health care for its population along with implementing economic reforms in the health sector. With the re-emergence of communicable diseases, HIV/ AIDS and its associated infections, the already existing gap between the need and access to health services increased (Arhin-Tenkorang, 2004; Gottret and Scieber, 2006).

Table 2.1

Characteristics of Different CBHI Models

No.	*Model*	*Beneficiary*	*Insurer*	*Provider*	*Subsidy by Govt.*	*Remarks*
1	Basic model	Members	CBHI society/ cooperative	Hospital	No	The members pay premium to the CBHI scheme, which in turn pays to the service provider for an assured set of services and the members whenever required can access the services .
2	Provider based model (Hospital based)	Members	Hospital	Hospital	No	The service provider offers a cashless system of health care for predefined sets of services decided collectively on a pre-payment basis for its members. The community or the members pay premium directly to the hospital on a monthly or yearly basis. The hospital manages the funds and provides the services to the members as and when required.
3	Where insurer is an NGO	Members	NGO/CBO	Partnered hospital	No	The NGO/CBO organises the community and initiates the insurance. The services availed can be cashless or on reimbursement basis. The NGO/ CBO negotiates with a set of independent service providers for certain set of services and based on average cost of the treatment and administrative cost, the premiums are collected from the community or members. The payment to the providers may be based on the number of users or fixed. In case of a cashless system, members can use the services directly from the providers and NGO/ CBO pays the fee directly to the providers.

contd...

...contd...

4	Third party managed CBHI	Members	NGO connected to a professional insurance company	Networked hospital	No	In this design, the NGO/CBO buys insurance coverage for its members from an insurance company for some specific services. The NGO collects the premium from the members and pays the premium to the insurance company for the services purchased. The negotiation with the service providers is the responsibility of the insurance company. The members can avail either the cashless option or be reimbursed by the service providers as notified by the insurance company for a fixed amount for fixed sets of services.
5	CBHI with inclusion of non-members in service provision	Members/Non-members with additional cost and only emergency service	NGO/CBO/CBHI society	Partnered hospital	No	It is not possible for CBHIs to achieve complete universal coverage for their target population due to various reasons like apprehension, inability to pay premium, and social stratification. Therefore, this resulted in many households remaining out of CBHI coverage. But whenever a medical emergency takes place, the non-members also seek services from the provider. To accommodate such non-members' demand for services, CBHIs generally modify their models giving them a limited coverage. In most of the cases, the provider charges a separate fee from non-members for the services utilised.

...contd...

6	CBHI with inclusion of non members and subsidised services	Members with dual benefit. Non-members with limited benefit	NGO/ CBO/CBHI society	Mainly public hospitals	Partly as public services are subsidised	This is the most common model for the CBHIs in Sub-Saharan African countries. In these countries, the CBHIs generally negotiate packaged rates with public for the utilisation of public funded services at a lower rate. In most of the eastern and southern African countries, the public health service system charge a high user fee from the user even after the subsidy provided by government. Therefore, in this model, the members of the schemes get a double subsidy. However, the non-members from CBHI area can utilise the services paying a differential price making it relatively costlier to the members but still cheaper to the normal cost.
7	CBHI with direct subsidy by government	Member	NGO/ CBO/CBHI society	Partnered hospital	Equal subsidy	This is a popular model in East Asia and some African countries where the government pays an equal amount to the premium paid by the members or to the total collected revenue. The costs of treatment in low and middle income countries are relatively high for the poor and marginalised section. The CBHI may not be able to give a comprehensive coverage to its members for the amount they pay as a premium. So by providing direct subsidy, the government is actually able to provide better services and also run a cost-shared health system.

Moreover, this period was marked by the increased involvement of the private sector in providing health care facilities. Baru (2003) shows that there in an incremental increase in the private health care facilities as well as the private bed strength across the countries in South Asia during the period of 1980-1995 when the economic reforms in health were first initiated.

Data show that the private expenditure and out-of-pocket (OOP) expenditure constituted a large proportion of the total health expenditure (WHO, 2009). The private expenditure in health constitutes almost 76 per cent of total expenditure in health and out of which almost 97 per cent is OOP health expenditure of developing and underdeveloping countries of Asia and Africa (WHO, 2009).

The higher private and external expenditure on health is not only affecting the national health services, but also directly impacts on the accessibility and affordability of health care. The introduction of reform strategies like user fees and contracting out of health facilities has reduced accessibility of the poor to the national health services system. The benefit of the health service system and the public spending on health were enjoyed primarily by the well-off population who can afford the services provided by the national health services system. Castro-Leal *et al.* (2000) in their study on seven countries in Africa show that poorer households reported less illness and seek lesser treatment from health care providers, although the frequency of illness is higher in this segment.

This inequality in access, need for universal coverage and provisioning of a comprehensive package of care forced governments, bilateral and multilateral agencies to promote CBHI in resource poor countries. Matul *et al.* (2010) show that in most of the countries where the social health insurance was not available or did not cover insurance need of the poor, the CBHI played an important, if not a substantial role.

As most of the developing countries share similar colonial characteristics and socio-economic indicators, the 'success' of CBHI schemes in African countries influenced the policy planner in other developing countries to adopt similar initiative in their respective countries. Over the years, CBHI became one of the major health service systems in the Afro-Asian region.

CBHI and Evidences of Success

Universal coverage of health services is one of the major thrust areas for the CBHIs. Most of the CBHIs aim to achieve universal coverage in their scheme area. Majority of the CBHI schemes are either facility based or geographical area based addressing the health needs and providing financial protection for a selected population group. The population groups are not homogeneous and are characterised by variations in socio-economic status. The stratification is generally at three levels (Houweling and Kunst, 2010): firstly, social stratification based on population sub-groups (tribe/caste), gender, religion, education, etc.; secondly, economic stratification based on individual and household income; and thirdly, geographical stratification based on the place of living. Therefore, it becomes imperative to study the CBHI schemes across the continent to see how CBHIs in Africa and Asia are addressing the issue of universal coverage. Basaza *et al.* (2009) in their review of CBHI of east Africa (Kenya, Uganda, Tanzania) show that coverage of the CBHI schemes are very negligible. In Kenya, the coverage was around 1 per cent of the total catchment population for the 30 CBHI schemes under review. In Uganda, the coverage was around 2 per cent from 12 scheme areas and in Tanzania the coverage was around 6 per cent from 77 CBHIs under study. At the level of a single scheme, no CBHI achieved more than 15 per cent coverage in its catchment population. Waelkens and Creil (as cited in Tabor, 2005) estimated the coverage at around 8 per cent of the targeted population in Sub-Saharan region. Musau (1999) estimated the coverage is in between 0.3 per cent and 6.5 per cent in their operating population. Arhin-Tenkorang (2004) puts the coverage of 6 major CBHI schemes in Africa as varying between 2 per cent and 66 per cent of the total targeted population.

Studies on CBHI in the South Asian region show a similar picture. Carrin *et al.* (2005) state that in Lalitpur scheme in Nepal, the coverage is about 48 per cent. The same review shows that the coverage of CBHI in Rwanda and Senegal is at 8 per cent and 37.4-

90.4 per cent respectively. In India, the coverage of the schemes are about 10 per cent to 50 per cent (Devadasan *et al.*, 2005) of the total target populations. The International Labour Office (ILO) Step (2005) document reviewed 51 schemes and came up with some absolute figure of individuals covered, but it does not give any proportional analysis of the coverage. The same study shows that almost 80 per cent of the CBHI schemes studied have a membership base of less than 100,000 and more than 33 per cent of all the schemes have coverage of less than 5,000. The study by Devadasan shows a similar figure with the Yeshaswini Scheme having more than 2.5 million members. Chankova (2008) puts the enrolment figure of schemes studied in West Africa between 2,200 and 46,500. Baeza *et al.* (2002) for ILO reviewed 258 CBHI schemes from Africa, Asia and Latin America. The review shows that 22 per cent of the CBHI has less than 100 members, 33 per cent has 100-500 members, 28 per cent has 500-10,000 members, 14 per cent has 10,000-100,000 members and only 2 per cent has more than 100,000 members. Moreover, the poorest of the poor are not included in the schemes and if the schemes have both rural and urban population, then generally the rural populations have less coverage.

Other major objective of CBHI is to ensure health equity and comprehensive care for the poor and marginalised by providing access to the health service system. As stated above, making health services accessible and affordable to the population is the major strategy to ensure health equity. Although most of the CBHIs try to design the schemes making it affordable and accessible to the poor, the data on coverage show that the actual number of people enrolling themselves in the schemes are still very small. The ILO study shows that out of 258 CBHIs reviewed, 146 schemes include outpatient service while 2 schemes included preventive care along with the OPD (outpatient department) services. In case of inpatient service, 146 schemes offer inpatient hospitalisation cost, and 3 CBHI schemes only offer inpatient facilities for basic maternity care. The cost of the medicines is covered by 131 CBHI schemes. Out of all the reviewed schemes, 121 CBHI schemes offer comprehensive coverage including outpatient, inpatient and cost of medicine, while rest of the schemes offer only selected services (Baeza *et al.*, 2002). The CAS (country assistance strategy) schemes in Burundi cover all inpatient care in the government clinics and hospitals. The Nkoranza schemes in Ghana and Community Health Fund in Tanzania cover the OPD services in any clinic, while inpatient services in selected registered facilities are covered. Abota schemes in Guinea-Bissau and Nkorazna scheme in Tanzania offer referral services. The coverage on cost of drugs depends upon the free or subsidised availability of the supplies. Many a times the patients have to buy drugs for the treatment (Arhin-Tenkorang, 2004a). The ACCORD (Action for Community Organisation, Rehabilitation and Development) schemes in India provide services at two levels. To certain members, it provides comprehensive coverage including preventive and promotive services, while the others have to pay for the medicine and a certain amount for hospitalisation (Devadasan *et al.*, 2004a). SEWA (Self Employed Women's Association) schemes offer predominantly primary care with limited hospitalisation benefit; whereas the health card system in Thailand offers both primary and secondary care (Bennett, 2004).

The need for medicine coverage is very important as it constitutes the largest share in OOP expenditure. Vialle-Valentin (2008) shows that most of the CBHI schemes do not give medicine cover to their members. The low membership, limited revenue collection, higher cost of branded drugs and non-availability of generic drugs supply to the health facilities make provisioning of the medicine unrealistic and non-viable for sustainability of the CBHI. The basic nature of comprehensiveness is compromised as the cost of the medicine has to be borne by the members. The non-medicine coverage is a reason for the low penetration of CBHI amongst the poorest as they have to bear the double burden by paying for premium of CBHI and the cost of medicine.

The above analysis shows that most of the CBHI schemes are not able to achieve universality in providing services. Even though the schemes operate in a local area, the coverage is still very low. The data on Asian schemes are limited as numbers of studies focused on the coverage of Asian schemes are also limited. The reason for the low coverage can be attributed to high premium for the coverage and individual member premium rather than household premium and no immediate benefit from the schemes (Devadassan *et al.*, 2005; Carrin *et al.*, 2005). Tabor (2005) and Bennett (2004) observed in their respective studies that the coverage in Asia is better than the coverage of the schemes in Africa. The studies by ILO and by Bennett show that the Asian CBHIs are larger and generally linked to a micro finance organisation which can give better financial security to the management of schemes (SEWA in India, Grameen in Bangladesh). By and large, the CBHIs in China have the largest memberships as in most of the schemes the membership is compulsory and most of these CBHIs in China are initiated by the government. The starting of cooperative movement in South East Asian countries also helps in creating larger CBHI schemes for its members as members of the cooperatives becomes automatically the members of CBHI. The issue with the African CBHIs, barring a few, is that most of the schemes are linked to hospitals or health facilities which have limited resources to cover the entire target population (Tabor, 2005). Moreover, the CBHIs in Africa are too dependent on external assistance. In Africa, more than 160 CBHI schemes are donor initiatives and dependent on the donor for the initial seed money. Between the years 2003-2006, some nine major donors invested over $10 million in CBHI schemes directly in a conservative calculation. The investment through the sub-grants and other associated health reforms grants were not taken into calculation as per USAID report (Chandani, 2008).

Inclusion of the poorest of the poor is another concern in estimating the memberships. Although the CBHIs aim to include all in their schemes, the poorest section is left out because of the obvious economic reason. The Nkorzana scheme's membership costs around 5-10 per cent of annual household expenditure; in Burundi 27 per cent of the community people could not afford the CBHI scheme as they cannot pay the premium (Bennett *et al.*, 1998). Designing special schemes for the poor requires more management and financial cost (Matul *et al.*, 2010). Therefore making the schemes viable, the poor are generally excluded.

At the time when the state is unable to provide quality essential care to the poor and marginalised and the market includes them according to their convenience in the insurance plan, CBHIs alone are able to mobilise resources, provide financial security and accessibility to health facilities and limit OOP expenditure. CBHI has been able to extend coverage to a large number of people who would otherwise not have financial protection (Jakab *et al.*, 2001). It also fills the gaps created by other health financing system both public and private in the process of transforming into a larger-scale system. As a part of this transformation, the health service system left out many groups or sections out of protection because of structural issues. The CBHI can serve these groups as an ad-hoc/intermediate system until the major system is ready to include the left out sections. However, protections provided by the CBHI are limited by its resource generation capacity. The services offered are directly proportional to the revenue generation capacity. The limitations in revenue generation raise the question of sustainability of these schemes. CBHI on certain occasions fails to provide services to the poorest of the poor, even though it is meant to cover them. The households which can afford to pay tend to dominate the CBHI membership and the marginalised who are unable to pay premium are left out (Gottret and Scieber, 2006).

Effectiveness of CBHI

Till date, 51 per cent of the poorest of the poor in Sub-Saharan Africa have had practically no medical coverage, not even CBHI coverage. In Lebanon where the health service system is almost run by private sector, the per capita cost on health care is more than double than that of Sri Lanka, where the health care sector is mostly public financed. But the coverage of Lebanese health care sector is half of what Sri Lankan health service system address. The concentration of private health care is mainly in urban areas and the health services provided by the private sector are mainly curative care at secondary or tertiary set-up. The failure of market to offer services to the poor and in the rural areas due to economic reasons is equally responsible for health inequity and reduced access to health. It is necessary to recognise that the markets too have failed to provide medical care to all, specially to the poor and marginalised. Interestingly in most of the literature, the success of public health service system providing better access and health care facilities is not documented. Study shows that most of the members of the CBHI schemes are generally the economically well-off section and the really poor are often left out (Carrin *et al.*, 2005; Ahuja and Jutthing, 2004). It is important that the health care needs of this section are addressed and included in health care coverage of the schemes. The designing of special packages for the people who cannot afford to pay the premium is the key to achieve universal coverage for the schemes.

CBHI is an instrument for ensuring access to health service to the population which is for any given reason left out from the health security network. It is the duty of the state, as per many universal declarations and covenants, to ensure health care services are made available to all. Therefore, the states should ensure that there is appropriate allocation of resources for the purchase of health services that ensures coverage for the entire population and decreasing OOP expenditure. CBHI cannot be a substitute nor is it a mechanism to prepare people to transit to the insurance-based schemes. CBHI should be essentially taken as an ad-hoc mechanism to ensure health service security for an intermediate period until the dominant health service system ensures health security to all. Treating CBHI as a substitute to a bigger health service may create more health inequity as the schemes are varied in nature. The benefit package, membership contribution and the financial protection of each and every CBHI are different, which in a larger context increases community-based health inequity.

Finally, the CBHI schemes should be able to adapt to changing patterns of demography, disease, costs, political will, expectations and technology, as all these factors have immense influence on the operation of any health service system. It is important that CBHI should be able to provide health security to the poor and the marginalised which are left out of the health services safety net and bring health equity in its true sense.

The Indian Experiment with Targeted Insurance

The Indian decision to follow mixed models of economy in its initial years of independence has manifested in the situation where both public and private service providers co-existed (Radhakrishna and Panda, 2006) before the shifts (as discussed above) in the health care financing paradigm. During 1990s when India decided to reform the economy and open its sectors, certain issues came up in the policy front. The government had to reduce its expenditure in the non-productive sectors and also ensure participation of the private sector in public provisioning of the services (Gupta, 2009).

This basic question brought the issues of alternative arrangement of health care finance to the forefront. The government policies as stated above started to emphasise on the model of health care financing which differentiate between the people who can afford to pay and who cannot pay for availing health care services (Ahuja, 2004a). Also, the official policies started defining the provisioning of public services and participation of private entities in health service delivery. These differentiations had a two-fold implication:

- The public health service delivery had become more targeted and shifted from a universal to insurance-based model.
- Opening up markets for private health insurance.

This dilemma can be seen in all the health and population policies adopted by the government post-1990s (Radhakrishna and Panda, 2006).

The formal genesis of the targeted health insurance model can be seen with the launch of The Universal Health insurance scheme by the union government in 2003 to provide universal health insurance coverage to below the poverty line (BPL) population in the age group of 3 months to 65 years. The scheme provided medical insurance coverage of ₹30,000 per year with maximum limit for one episode of illness of ₹15,000. The coverage is based on the annual premium of ₹365 for individual, ₹548 for a family of five and ₹730 for a family of seven. The benefit of the scheme was limited to cases of hospitalisation only and did not include outpatient care. The treatment costs are reimbursed to the hospital by the insurance companies according to previously fixed rates (Rao, 2005).

During 2004, the government also provided health insurance coverage of ₹10,000 for the self-help groups (SHGs) on the payment of ₹200 premium (Rao, 2005).

The 11th Five Year Plan promoted the idea for a health insurance, which mentions the need to protect the poor as there is a need to secure their health in the current scenario of rising costs and inequitable provision of services. The Plan documents pointed to the evidence from the 60th round of National Sample Survey Organisation (NSSO) that cost of hospitalisation at public hospitals in rural areas of India stands at ₹3,000 per episode of hospitalisation, which is up to ₹7,000 in case of private institutions.[2] The same considered in the urban areas is at ₹11,000 at private hospitals and is almost 3 times higher than the rates of public hospitals. In this context, the Plan document proposes to introduce comprehensive health care insurance on a risk sharing basis for all and 'particularly for the poor.'[3]

Interestingly, social health insurance in India has been largely restricted to the organised sector that constitutes only a small proportion of the population. It has been estimated that social health insurance supports only 2 per cent of the population in India and almost 18 per cent is supported by the government budgetary insurance schemes (Rao, 2005).

The section on health insurance for the unorganised sector of the 11th Plan states the idea and the will to introduce:

> ...new scheme based on cashless transaction with the objective of improving access to health care and protecting the individual and their family from exorbitant out-of-pocket expenses. Under this scheme, coverage will be given to the beneficiary and her family of five members. Providers will be both public and private.[4]

The Common Minimum Programme (CMP) of the United Progressive Alliance (UPA) Government in 2004 promised to meet the growing demand for health care and to start a national health

2. NSSO 60th Round is available at Ministry of Statistics and Programme Implementation website at *http://mospi.gov.in/national_data_bank/ndb-rpts.htm.*
3. Eleventh Five Year Plan document is available at Planning Commission website at *http://planningcommission.nic.in/plans/planrel/fiveyr/welcome.html* as accessed on 12/11/2011.
4. Ibid.

insurance scheme for the BPL families, who might be pushed into the debt trap in case of hospitalisation or a prolonged illness. The CMP came up with a new scheme where workers in the unorganised sector would be covered under the scheme and they would be benefited in case of emergencies and illnesses. The approach was a targeted one covering those who live below the poverty line, earning their livelihood by being employed in the informal sector with no job guarantees or savings to fall back upon during times of distress.[5]

The Rashtriya Swasthya Bima Yojana (RSBY) scheme was announced in the year 2007 by Prime Minister Dr Manmohan Singh, under the aegis of the Ministry of Labour. The actual rollout of the scheme started in the year 2008 (Rajasekhar *et al.*, 2011) in a phased manner throughout the country, aiming to cover the entire nation by the year 2012-13. It was launched by the Ministry of Labour, Government of India (GoI), to provide health insurance for workers belonging to unorganised sector falling below the BPL as a part of the Unorganised Workers Social Security Act of 2008. The scheme has financial coverage of ₹30,000 for a family of five, which can be claimed in a year, in case of illness involving hospitalisation. Beneficiaries are required to pay only ₹30 as registration fee while Central and state governments pay the premium to the insurer selected by the state governments on the basis of a competitive bidding. Presently, the scheme has been extended to all citizens who belong to the BPL category. The targeted beneficiaries have to make sure to enrol themselves under the scheme and also to complete the registration procedure by giving their thumb impression at the time of registration. In the financial year 2010-11, the scheme has been expanded also to include Mahatma Gandhi National Rural Employment Gurantee Act (MGNREGA) workers. Thus paving way for state sponsored targeted health insurance which closely follows the genesis of community-based targeted health insurance in terms of conceptualisation and design.

5. National Common Minimum Programme of Government of India, 2004, available at *http://pmindia.nic.in/cmp.pdf* as accessed on 10/01/2012.

References

Ahuja, R. (2004). "Health Insurance for the Poor", *Economic and Political Weekly*: 3171–78, July 10.

———. (2004a). "Health Insurance for the Poor in India", *Working Paper* No. 123. New Delhi: Indian Council for Research on International Economic Relations.

Ahuja, R. and J. Jutthing (2004). "Are the Poor too Poor to Demand Health Insurance?", *Journal of Microfinance* 6(1): 1-20.

Akin, John S., Nancy Birdsall and David M. De Ferranti (1987). *Financing Health Service in Developing Countries*. Washington DC, USA: Policy and Research Division, The World Bank.

Arhin-Tenkorang, D. (2004). "Experience of Community Health Financing in the Asian Region", in A.S. Preker and Guy Carrin (eds.), *Health Financing for Poor People: Resource Mobilization and Risk Sharing*. Washington: World Bank.

Arhin- Tenkorang, D. (2004a) "Experience of Community Health Financing in African Region", in A.S. Preker and Guy Carrin (eds.), *Health Financing for Poor People: Resource Mobilization and Risk Sharing*. Washington: World Bank. Chapter 4.

Baeza, C., Fernando Montenegro and Marco Nunez (2002). *Extending Social Protection in Health through Community-based Health Organization*. Geneva: Universitas Programme, International Labour Office.

Baru, R. (2003). "Privatization of Health Services: A South Asian Perspective", *Economic and Political Weekly* 38(42): 4433-37.

Basaza, Robert, George Pariyo and Bart Criel (2009). "What are the Emerging Features of Community Health Insurance Schemes in East Africa", *Risk Management and Health care Policy* 2: 47–53.

Bennett, S. (2004). "The Role of Community-Based Health Insurance within the Health Care Financing System: A Framework for Analysis", *Health Policy and Planning* 19(3): 147–58.

Bennett, S., A. Creesa and R. Monasch. (1998). "Health Insurance for People Outside Formal Sector Employment", *APA Paper* No. 16. Geneva: WHO.

Bloom, G. (2001). "Equity in Health in Unequal Societies: Meeting Health Needs in Contexts of Social Change", *Health Policy* 57: 205-24.

Bonilla-Chachin, M., E. Murrugarra and M. Temourov (2003). *Health Care During Transition and Health Systems Reform: Evidence from Poorest CIS Countries*. Lucerne Conference of the CIS-7 Initiative. January 20-22. Switzerland.

Brugha, R. and A.B. Zwi (2002). "Global Approaches to Private Sector Provision: Where is the Evidence?", in Kelley Lee, Kent Buse and Suzanne Fustukian (eds.), *Health Policy in a Globalizing World*. Cambridge, UK: The Cambridge University Press.

Carrin, G., M.P. Waelkens and B. Criel (2005). "Community Based Health Insurance in Developing Countries: A Study of its Contribution to the Performance of Health Financing System", *Tropical Medicine and International Health* 10(8): 799–811.

Castro-Leal, F., J. Dayton, L. Demery and K. Mehra (2000). "Public Spending in Health in Africa: Do the Poor Benefit", *Bulletin of the World Health Organization* 78(1): 66-74.

Chandani, T. (2008). *Lessons Learned and Recommendations for Donors Supporting Micro Insurance*. USA: USAID/CGAP Working Group on Micro Insurance.

Chankova, S. (2008). "Impact of Mutual Health Organizations: Evidence from West Africa", *Health Policy and Planning* 23: 264–76.

Devadasan, N., Kent Ranson, Wim van Damme and Bart Criel (2004). "Community Health Insurance in India: An Overview", *Economic and Political Weekly*: 3170-83, 10 July

Devadasan, N.S., Manoharan, N. Memon, S. Menon, M. Thekaekara, S, Thekaekara and AMS Team (2004a). "ACCORD Community Health Insurance Increasing Access to Hospital Care", *Economic and Political Weekly*: 3189-94, 10 July.

Drouin, A. (2007). *Methods of Financing Health Care : A Rational Use of Financing Mechanisms to Achieve Universal Coverage*. Technical Commission on Statistical, Actuarial and Financial Studies World Social Security Forum, Moscow. 10-15 September.

Gottret, P. and G. Scieber (2006). *Health Finance Revisited*. Washington DC: The World Bank.

Gupta, I. (2009). *Out-of-Pocket Expenditures and Poverty: Estimates from NSS 61st Round*. Paper presented for to the Expert Group on Poverty. Planning Commission. 12 May.

Haddad, S., E. Bans and D. Narayana (eds.) (2008). *Safeguarding the Health Sector in Times of Macroeconomic Instability: Policy Lessons for Low- and Middle-Income Countries*. New Jersey: Africa World Press. Chapter 1.

Houweling, Tanja A.J. and Anton E. Kunst (2010). "Socio-economic Inequalities in Childhood Mortality in Low- and Middle-income Countries: A Review of the International Evidence", *British Medical Bulletin* 93: 7–26.

ILO (2005). *India: An Inventory of Micro Insurance Schemes*. Geneva: Strategies and Tools against Social Exclusion and Poverty (Step) Programme.

Jakab, M., A.S. Preker, C. Krishnan, P. Schneider, F. Diop, J. Jutting, A. Gumber, K. Ranson and S. Supakankunti (2001). "Social Inclusion and Financial Protection through Community Financing", *Health, Nutrition, and Population Discussion Paper*. Washington DC: The World Bank.

Lee, K. and H. Goodman (2002). "Global Policy Network: The Propagation of Health Care Financing Reforms since 1980", in Kelley Lee, Kent Buse and Suzanne Fustukian (eds.), *Health Policy in a Globalizing World*. Cambridge, UK: The Cambridge University Press.

Musau, S. (1999). *Community-based Health Insurance: Experiences and Lessons Learned from East Africa*. USA: Partnerships for Health Reform Project, Abt Associate.

Matul, Michal, Michael J. McCord, Caroline Phily and Job Harms (2010). *The Landscape of Micro Insurance in Africa*. Geneva: International Labour Office.

Ollila, E. (2005). "Global Health Priorities: Priorities of the Wealthy?", *Globalization and Health*.

Radhakrishna, R. and M. Panda (2006). *Macroeconomics of Poverty Reduction: India Case Study*. Mumbai: Indira Gandhi Institute of Development Research.

Rajasekhar, D., Erlend Berg, Maitreesh Ghatak, R. Manjula and Sanchari Roy (2011). "Implementing Health Insurance for the Poor: The Rollout of RSBY in Karnataka", *Discussion Paper Series* EOPP/2011/25, Economic Organisation and Public Policy Programme, Suntory and Toyota International Centres for Economics and Related Disciplines (STICERD), London School of Economics and Political Science. Available at *www.sticerd.lse.ac.uk/dps/eopp/eopp25.pdf* (accessed on 23/02/2012).

Rao, K.S. (2005). *Health Insurance in India, Financing and Delivery of Health Care Services in India*. National Commission on Macroeconomics and Health. Ministry of Health & Family Welfare Government of India.

Tabor, S. (2005). *Community-based Health Insurance and Social Protection Policy*. Washington DC: Human Development Network, The World Bank.

Tritter, J.Q., M. Koivusalo, E. Ollila and P. Dorfman (2010). *Globalization Market and Health Care Policy: Rewarding the Patient as Consumer*. London: Routledge.

Tuohy, C.H., Colleen M. Flood and Marl Stabile (2004). "How Does Private Finance Affect Public Health Care Systems? Marshalling the Evidence from OECD Nations", *Journal of Health Politics, Policy and Law* 29(3): 359-96.

Vialle-Valentin, C. (2008). "Medicines Coverage and Community-based Health Insurance in Low-Income Countries", *Health Research Policy and Systems* 6:11.

Wanke, M.I., L.D. Saunders, R.W. Pong and W.J.B. Church (1995). *Building a Stronger Foundation: A Framework for Planning and Evaluating Community-based Health Services in Canada.* Ottawa: Health Canada. p.8.

WHO (2000). *The World Health Report 2000: Health Systems: Improving Performance.* Geneva.

————. (2007). *Everybody Business: Strengthening Health Systems to Improve Health Outcomes: WHO's Framework.* Geneva: WHO Press.

————. (2009). *World Health Statistics, 2009.* WHO Statistical Information System (WHOSIS).

Zwi, A.B. and A. Mills (1995). "Health Policy in Less Developed Countries: Past Trends and Future Directions", *Journal of International Development* 7(3): 299-328, May-June.

3

ARCHANA DIWATE

Medical Insurance for Informal Workers

Case of Waste Pickers in Pune, Maharashtra

Introduction

The last two decades have witnessed an increasing commercialisation and weakening of public health provisioning. Today, the major crisis that India's health services face is that of financing health care and uneven distribution of health care resources. The state continues to play an important role in the financing and provisioning of health care. Health services in themselves play a critical role in reducing inequities or perpetuating existing inequities and it also shapes the existing patterns of health services (Gilson *et al.*, 2007). The growing inequities in health outcomes due to inequalities in accessibility, availability and affordability of health care at the national level, across states and as well as within socio-economic groups are widely observed and studied (GoI, 2002a; NSSO, 2006; IIPS and Macro International, 2007). The National Health Policy of 2002 and the utilisation data of NSSO (2006), show that there is greater reliance on the private sector. As a result, the cost of care has increased tremendously (GoI, 2002a; NSSO, 2006).

It is a well-known fact that public health expenditure is minimal thereby the quality of public health care deteriorated to a large extent (Baru *et al.*, 2010). The last few decades have witnessed an increased commercialisation of public health services and tremendous expansion of the private health sector (Duggal, 2005). These changes have forced majority of India's poor to access expensive private health care that has resulted in high out-of-pocket (OOP) expenditure. Indebtedness due to rising cost of health care has increased and there is also evidence that shows high cost of medical care is an important reason for not seeking treatment especially among the lower income quintile (Krishnan, 1999; Baru, 1999; Dilip, 2005; Ellis *et al.*, 2000; Duggal, 2005). These factors result in the poor getting excluded from accessing health care despite them being the neediest (Hart, 2000).

In the context of rising costs of medical care and decreasing access to health care, workers involved in the informal sector who constitute the majority of the marginalised and vulnerable groups are worst affected (Gumber and Kulkarni, 2000).

One of the measures to address this problem of increasing cost and inaccessibility to health services is through the introduction of medical insurance schemes especially for the vulnerable sections of the society. These have been initiated by the government, NGOs (non-governmental organisations) in partnership with insurance companies and private hospitals and also by the trade unions. There has been a plurality of these schemes, each shaped by different socio-political contexts.

The present paper is based on a qualitative study of the medical insurance scheme initiated by the waste pickers union in Pune. In order to understand the medical insurance scheme and its experiences, in-depth interviews were conducted with key informants. These included the members of the union, TPA (Third Party Agency) and the beneficiaries. It also focused on secondary sources, including reports, micro level studies and published articles of the organisation which have been referred to and analysed. The paper presents the design of the medical insurance scheme, its functioning and experiences of waste pickers who have been beneficiaries of the medical insurance scheme.

Waste Pickers as a Category of Informal Workers

The National Commission for Enterprises in the Unorganised Sector (NCEUS) has observed that over 92 per cent of workforce are engaged in the informal sector. Over the last few decades, there has been a tremendous growth in the informal sector as well as in the informalisation of labour in the formal sector. It is observed that even though India has gained massive economic growth, its benefits have not penetrated to the people who are part of the informal sector (NCEUS, 2007). These workers are individuals who do not come under any legal protection. They are deprived of essential social security measures such as provident fund, pension, maternity and health care benefits and paid leave for sickness. There is little or no work security, compounded by the lack of organising powers for the formation of trade unions, thereby reducing their bargaining power in improving or bringing about changes in their working conditions. It is also important to remember that this sector is very wide and diverse in nature, their characteristics and the activities undertaken by them. Poor working conditions accompanied by low wages and the lack of employment security thus make these workers more vulnerable (Holmstrom, 1985; Breman, 2010).

The social characteristics of workers in the informal sector are that they are concentrated in the bottom rung of work and social hierarchy (Holmstrom, 1985; Breman, 2010; Qadeer and Roy, 1989; NCEUS, 2007). It is important to understand that historically, most of the informal workers belong to the socially and economically excluded sections of society and therefore end up as a part of the informal sector. Develtere and Durme (1999-2000: 68) state that "the existence of the informal sector is a consequence of the exclusion of many social groups." The NCEUS (2009) report highlighted that in the end of 2004-05, 77 per cent (836 million) of the people were living below the official poverty line and around 79 per cent of the informal workers belonged to this group. It is also evident that those who are economically and socially marginalised get less access to health services (Krishnan, 1999; Sen *et al.*, 2007; Baraik and Kulkarni, 2006).

Within the informal sector, waste pickers occupy the lowest position socially and economically. Across cities in developing countries, millions of people are dependent on the collection and sale of waste for their survival and livelihood. Waste pickers belong to the bottom of hierarchy of waste collection and rank lowest in the urban informal economy (GoI, 2002b). The key push factor that forces waste pickers to engage in this type of work is poverty and renders them invisible from the mainstream society and economy (Medina, 2005). Their work is considered as 'dirty' and thereby looked down upon. Waste pickers' experience shows that they are exploited and discriminated by society and its institutions of authority such as police and guards. Samson (2009: 1) observes that "they are frequently ignored within public policy processes and harassed and persecuted by authorities." According to Medina (2007, as cited in Samson, 2009: 1), "the World Bank estimates that one per cent of the world's population, or fifteen million people, earn their livelihood from these activities."

A description of the various tasks undertaken by them has been summarised by Kuria and Muasya (2010: 3) who observed that:

> Waste pickers collect and dispose of waste by collecting, using and selling reusable or recyclable materials, and disposing of what they cannot sell in a variety of ways. Waste is collected from houses, restaurants, hotels, markets and streets. Waste pickers are paid directly by their clients and also make money from sales of recyclables and other items. Waste pickers can be street dwellers (homeless), youths or families. They may work as individuals, or organised as self-help groups (SHGs), community-based organisations (CBOs), non-governmental organisations (NGOs), networks, associations or cooperatives.

Most of the studies have observed that waste pickers belong to the marginalised and vulnerable sections of the society mostly as poor people, women, children and migrants. They live in precarious conditions in urban slums. The literacy level is very low among these waste pickers. For example, in India, they belong to the untouchable castes as Dalit and among the Dalits, this task has been done by the Mang and Mahar communities.[1] Along with hostile social status, the living and extremely hazardous working conditions exposes them to multiple and constant health risks (Wilson *et al.*, 2006; Cointreau, 2006; Sarkar, 2003; Chikarmane and Narayan, 2005; Hayami *et al.*, 2003; Hunt, 1996).

They are unprotected and deprived of basic facilities such as safe drinking water, sanitation, housing, health services, etc. (Chintan, 2003 cited in Chikarmane and Narayan, 2009). The multiple facets of deprivation on the basis of caste along with poor economic conditions

1. These groups are in Maharashtra.

and low literacy levels increase their vulnerability. Therefore, this category of worker in the informal sector experiences social exclusion that translates into an inability to participate in social and economic spheres of everyday life (Thorat and Sabharwal, 2010). The work environment of the waste pickers is characterised by unfavourable conditions. Many times while collecting waste on roads or garbage bins or segregating it, they come into daily contact with several kinds of biological waste material including dead rat, cat or other animal, human faeces, hides, etc., which exposes them to health risks such as severe infections (Chikarmane and Narayan, 2009; SNDT and Chintan, 2008). Studies have pointed out that anaemia, tuberculosis and under nutrition are common health problems among the waste pickers and as a result they are more susceptible to occupational health hazards. Cuts in the hand due to handling glass, metal sharps and broken bottles as well as accidents are very common injuries among the waste pickers. A major health problem reported by waste pickers is back pain due to the constant bending motion required to search for waste (Cointreau, 2006; Hunt, 1996; Nguyen *et al.*, 2011). It has been also noted that injuries due to medical wastes are more dangerous "because the waste pickers maybe unknowingly get infected by Hepatitis B and C or HIV or other bacterial infections through contaminated sharps and needles" (Sarkar, 2003: 8). It is seen most often that these health needs of the waste pickers are neglected. Moreover, the rising cost of health care pushes informal waste pickers into a debt crisis, thereby increases their impoverishment.

In India, medical insurance is a very recent phenomenon and the coverage of medical insurance in the country is very limited, covering only 10 per cent of the total population (Mavalankar and Bhat, 2000). The Central Government Health Scheme (CGHS) and Employees' State Insurance Scheme (ESIS) that were established in 1954 and 1948 are available only for the central and state government workers respectively, who are mostly in organised or formal sectors. Private medical insurance schemes offer different packages, but these schemes are mainly for those people who have ability to pay for it (GoI, 2006, cited in Baru *et al.*, 2010). In all these insurance schemes, the worker in the informal sector gets excluded.

As an appropriate strategy to reduce health care burden on the poor, the Community-based Medical Insurance (CBMI) received increasing attention from policy makers since the 1990s (Carrin *et al.*, 2005). It got recognition mainly in developing countries where public health facilities are poor and large sections of the society have a low payment capacity (Rao, 2005). The characteristics of CBMI scheme is 'not for profit' and based on the principle of risk sharing and community involvement. It is meant for poor people who are working in the informal sector. Risk sharing and pooling of resources protect people from the unexpected health expenditure and facilitate accessing medical care. "By pooling resources, health insurance schemes can improve equity of and access to health care and can offer financial protection" (Ranson, 2002: 614).

In India, CBMI has a plurality of approaches as NGOs, trade unions, cooperatives and SHGs have initiated CBHI Schemes with involvement of the community, insurance companies and providers (Devadasan *et al.*, 2004).

It is within this context that a medical insurance scheme was initiated by the waste pickers union in Pune. The objective of this initiative was to protect waste pickers' from the debt due to the rising cost of health care. The union was formally registered in 1993 and have stared insurance scheme in 2003 through negotiations with Pune Municipal Corporation (PMC). It was cost effective for the PMC to provide medical insurance to waste pickers who were informal workers by paying the annual premium rather than employ full-time workers. This motivated the PMC to partner in the launching of the medical insurance scheme.

Medical Insurance Scheme for Municipal Workers in Pune: Eligibility, Inclusion and Exclusion

The New India Assurance Company was selected as the official insurer for the waste pickers' union, and a scheme was started under the social insurance scheme of the company called Jan Arogya Bima Policy. The insurance scheme started in 2003 with an enrolment of 3,707 members that increased to 5,411 members in 2007 (Ahmed,

2007) and 6,555 in 2010.[2] In this insurance scheme, the trade union of waste pickers acts as a channel and bridge between the PMC, insurance company and the beneficiary. The entire annual premium of all registered waste pickers is being paid by the PMC. The members who have joined the union and have taken the membership card are automatically covered under this medical insurance scheme. It is a reimbursement scheme, and at the time of hospitalisation, the patients or beneficiaries have to pay from their pocket and then later claim the amount spent (Scott, 2010).

The Eligibility and Inclusion Criteria

Only the members of the union of waste pickers (Kagad Kach Patra Kashtakari Panchayat [KKPKP], Pune) can avail benefits of the scheme. The union members are 6,555 currently[3] and 90 per cent of them are women. The age of eligibility is between 18-70 years old.[4]

The criteria for selection of hospitals are that it should be a registered hospital and have the required facilities for indoor treatment.[5] However, the union negotiated with the insurer to waive the minimum bed requirement of 15 beds as waste pickers are too poor and generally prefer to go to the nearest hospitals, which are small and may not fulfil the required bed criteria. Many waste pickers take treatment on credit because of their good relationship with the local doctor (Ahmed, 2007).

The conditions for making a claim include the notification to be given within seven days of the date of hospitalisation to the insurance company and the particulars of the claim must be filed within 30 days from the date of discharge from the hospital.[6]

---

2. The information collected from the assistant of the Solid Waste Management Department of PMC, 17 December 2010.
3. Ibid.
4. The information collected from the Administrative Officer at New India Assurance Company Ltd., on phone, 29 December 2010.
5. Prospectus of Jan Arogya Bima Policy, New India Assurance Company Ltd.
6. Ibid.

Coverage: The reimbursement amount is ₹5,000 for a period of one year. It covers hospitalisation if it is more than or at least for 24 hours.

Exclusion Criteria: This medical insurance scheme is only provided to the individual worker and does not include family members. It does not cover outpatient care and only covers hospitalisation. Any pre-existing illness is not covered under this scheme. The scheme defines pre-existing condition as 'any disease, or symptoms' of any illness and injury which existed prior to the effective date of this insurance. It also stated that any expenditure on hospitalisation that occurred within 30 days of the commencement date of the insurance would be excluded, except in the case of injury arising due to an accident. Dental treatments or surgery of any kind unless requires hospitalisation, convalescence, general disability, 'run down' condition or rest cure, venereal diseases, congenital external diseases, sterility and HIV/AIDS are such diseases that are excluded from the coverage. Expenses on vitamins and tonics, treatments arising from or traceable to pregnancy/child birth inclusion of caesarean section are also excluded. During the first year of operation of insurance cover, the expenses on treatment of diseases such as cataract, benign prostatic hypertrophy, hysterectomy for menorrhagia or fibromyoma, hernia, hydrocele, congenital internal diseases, fistula in anus, piles, sinusitis and related disorders are not payable.[7]

Operationalisation of the Scheme

At the time of illness, patient has to inform the union about any hospitalisation. Then the union conveys this message to the insurance company. Initially, the patient has to pay from their pocket and within 30 days they are supposed to claim for the reimbursement with all the documents. The claim procedure, scrutinising it and keeping all the records and then forwarding it to the insurance company—all these procedures are done at the level of union. Then the insurance company scrutinises the claims and gives the reimbursement money

7. Prospectus of Jan Arogya Bima Policy, New India Assurance Company Ltd .

to the union. And the union distributes the reimbursement money to the claimants.

Figure 3.1

The Design of the Medical Insurance Scheme

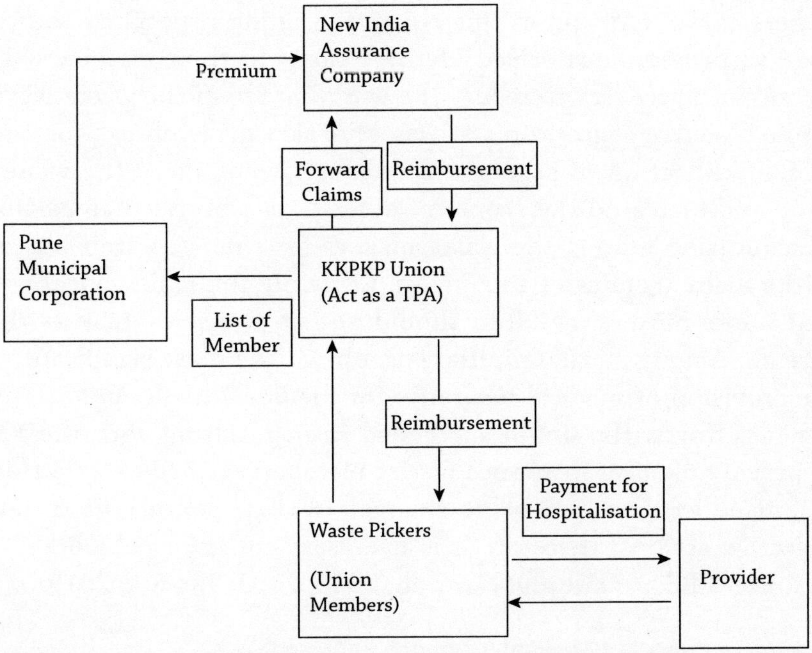

The Main Actors in the Medical Insurance Scheme

Three main actors are involved in the implementation of the medical insurance scheme.

1. The Union.
2. Municipal Corporation (State).
3. Insurance Company.
4. The Waste Picker as Beneficiary.

Role of the Waste Pickers' Union in Initiation of the Insurance Scheme

The case of waste pickers' union in Pune is a successful example of organising informal workers. The important feature of this union is to make the state accountable for providing basic services to informal workers. The waste pickers' union has struggled to improve the working conditions of their members and has taken up many initiatives for the upgradation and enhancement of livelihoods of the waste pickers. Firstly, they took initiative to recognise the waste pickers as workers and in this regard the union negotiated with the PMC to provide authorised identity cards to their members. The second initiative was to reduce the work burden of the waste pickers through source segregation of waste. It also made efforts for door-to-door collection of segregated waste that enhanced the value of scrap and increased the economic security of workers. Campaigning for education among the waste pickers for their children was one of the main agendas of this union. Certainly the main concern was that waste pickers' children should not do the same task as their parents. Among all these initiatives, one of the most significant was the provision of medical insurance for members of the union. After several efforts, the union succeeded in negotiating with the PMC to provide medical insurance for its members. It believed that only organised workers can bring changes in their conditions through collective actions; therefore it is necessary for informal workers to organise (Chikarmane and Narayan, 2000; 2005; Tamara, 2010).

Why Union Promoted Medical Insurance Scheme

The extremely hazardous working condition of waste pickers exposes them to many health-related problems, and this vulnerability increases due to poverty and lack of access to resources. Many a times, waste pickers cannot afford the cost of the treatment. This argument was substantiated by the union on the basis of two studies that has been conducted by the union members. One of the studies conducted in 2000 on behalf of the International Labour Organisation (ILO) by a team of researchers of SNDT Women University gave an opportunity to quantify the contribution of different actors at different levels in the informal waste sector. It revealed that the municipality was gaining financially from waste pickers. This was due to savings of nearly ₹16 million per annum on transportation costs incurred for collection of waste alone. This is because they collect the waste and save the transportation costs of the municipality (Chikarmane *et al.*, 2001, cited in Chikarmane and Narayan, 2005). Another small sample study of waste pickers in Pune conducted by the union members observed some patterns of illness as reported by the waste pickers. The major reported illnesses were severe musculo-skeletal problems, injuries due to falling from or into garbage bins, respiratory tract infections and gastrointestinal ailments, occupation-related accidents, tuberculosis and eye infections. It was observed that waste pickers, particularly women, tended to ignore minor illnesses till they assumed dangerous proportions and became chronic 'conditions' (Chikarmane *et al.*, 2001, cited in SNDT and Chintan Environmental Research and Action Group, 2008: 49). The union argued that it is the prime responsibility of the PMC to protect the marginalised sections of the society to which the waste pickers mostly belonged. Based on the findings of both these studies, the union recommended that waste pickers should be considered as 'unprotected workers' and the Municipality should provide some welfare benefits such as life and medical insurance to them. This evidence led the union to demand for medical insurance from the municipality, and after two years of constant struggle, the collective voice of the waste pickers was heard and ended successfully. In 2003, PMC agreed to provide medical insurance to all the registered waste pickers, thus becoming the first municipality in the country to provide medical insurance scheme for the waste pickers on payment of an annual premium (Chikarmane and Narayan, 2005).

Municipal Corporation Role

It is also important to understand the role of the PMC and the motive behind providing medical insurance scheme to the waste pickers. The PMC is actually on benefit side, even though they provide annual premium of the medical insurance scheme. Because the total premium cost of all members that PMC is paying is very small, amounting to around ₹0.5 million. On the other hand, the waste pickers are saving the cost of PMC at around ₹16 million annually (Chikarmane and Narayan, 2005). Thus, the PMC's grant appears as mere tokenism to the waste pickers. Moreover, the PMC is availing the labour of these waste pickers through doorstep collection of waste, but not providing them with any regular employment or social security. It clearly shows that how the state e.g., PMC is reducing its responsibility by keeping these workers in the informal sector.

Insurance Company

Insurance company also takes interest in providing medical insurance packages even though they start this insurance scheme under the umbrella of social health insurance. The study conducted by Ahmed (2007) on the same insurance scheme shows that the payout is lower than the premium paid.

Table 3.1

Premium to Payout Trend

Year	*2003*	*2004*	*2005*	*2006*	*Total (Grand)*
Premium paid	2,92,140	2,54,210	3,30,680	3,63,720	12,40,750
Claim amount Disbursed (Payout)	89,953	2,71,995	3,09,365	2,65,862	9,37,175

Source: Ahmed, 2007: 43.

Table 3.1 clearly shows that in all years except 2004 the payout is lower than the premium paid. This means the total premium paid by the PMC is higher compared to claim amount disbursed. In a period of four years (2003-2006), the insurance company has benefited financially at the tune of around ₹3,03,575. This indicates that the insurance company is financially gaining as the claim rates are low.

The Waste Picker as Beneficiary

The role of a insured worker is to claim the money which was borne at the time of hospitalisation. The worker has to fill up the claim form with all documents such as medicines bills, diagnostic test bills, discharge card, etc., and then has to submit to the union.

Experiences of Waste Pickers as Beneficiaries

In this section, recent ailments for which waste pickers have claimed the benefit of medical insurance are studied. This section tries to get a comprehensive view about the experiences of people in availing the medical insurance facility. This was done through asking questions about their ailments, their institutional treatment seeking behaviour, experiences about insurance claim and reimbursement procedure.

Health Problems and Choice of Provider

The waste pickers' experiences explained that the injuries due to broken glass or metal are very common and have to face such problems in their daily life. The other experiences that the waste pickers mentioned include back pain and pain in joints as major problems for them as a result of carrying heavy load of collected waste and walking long distances. These problems are high among those workers who are working on the streets, walking long distances in search for waste. The workers engaged in door-to-door collection have lesser workload but face similar problems as they were working on streets before they began door-to-door collection.

Injuries due to accidents are also one of the major problems faced by waste pickers. One of the waste pickers reported that she had an accident when she was working on the streets and collecting waste. Since then, she has not been able to work properly and cannot work for long hours. The health problems cited by the waste pickers pose serious concerns about their occupational health hazards.

Although they suffer from many ailments, their economic conditions do not permit them to seek medical help. That is why they do not prefer to go to the doctor for such daily pains and sufferings. First response to any physical suffering is to avoid it. They do not give importance to minor illness as they believe that it is a part and parcel of life of any waste picker. The rationale for such behaviour is the cost involved for accessing medical care, which they cannot afford. Waste pickers' experiences showed that the rising cost of medical care makes access to health services difficult.

They prefer to buy medicines over the counter, and if there are wounds or injuries due to broken glass, then they just put *chunna*[8]

8. *Chunna* is white paste of calcium generally used with chewing tobacco.

on that wound or they keep that wound open and continue to work. In the life of a waste picker, only serious illnesses perceived as direct threat to loss of wages and life are worthy of attention and medical care.

Waste pickers' experiences explained that generally they do not pay attention to routine problems such as minor injuries which are regarded as a part of their lives. The income and the high medical cost stand as obstacles in dealing with majority of health problems. It is not the case that they are not willing to treat these health problems, but the fact is that medical care is not within their reach.

When asked about the choice of provider i.e., where they take treatment when they fall ill, the waste pickers' explicit responses were that they prefer to go to the private clinic. The most common reason for choosing private clinic was the proximity. Most of the waste pickers said that it is easily accessible because it is closer to their houses and they do not have to lose their daily wages. Easy access, availability of doctor at convenient time and proximity make these clinics an easy choice. The ultimate aim is to save wages. Another reason to choose these clinics is the relationship with the provider. They trust the private doctors because these doctors also provide services on credit. The waste pickers do not prefer government hospitals because if they take into account the direct and indirect costs involved, then it is as much as a private hospital. Moreover, they believe that quality of care is poor in a government hospital. A similar observation was found in a study conducted by Ahmed (2007: 48) where most of the members accessed private hospitals because of proximity and faith in the doctor, flexibility in payment mechanism and quality of care. The waste pickers mentioned a number of other reasons than just the cost consideration for not choosing government hospitals. They cited reasons such as the long waiting line for the doctors, unfair treatment by doctors and other medical staff, and non-availability of medicine. The levels of discrimination in the health services have been noted by Acharya (2010: 35) who states that:

> If the interaction with the provider is restricted due to use of derogatory words and refrain from touch (or offending touch) during

diagnosis, counselling, pathological test or while seeking referral, there is a likelihood that the required health care will not reach the user.

Experience of Medical Insurance Scheme

The workers' experiences indicate that the union had taken great efforts in reducing the economic burden due to health expenditures; however it does not fulfil their needs of health care and does not ease their economic burden completely. The medical insurance scheme is a reimbursement scheme and the insurance benefit offered is very minimal in the context of rising costs of health care. It is found that the workers are well aware about the claim procedure as all respondents claimed reimbursement at some point. The experience of workers shows that arranging money for payment to the health facility is a huge problem and a difficult task.

Waste pickers said that the benefit amount is inadequate, and therefore it does not provide any financial security in case of a health incident. The main reason is that since this is a reimbursement scheme, at the time of illness they have to pay the amount for treatment. There is no escape from it and to pay that hospitalisation expenditure they have to take money on loan or sell their assets. A 20-year old waste picker said that:

> When illness occurs we have to pay for the treatment. The "health bima" (medical insurance benefit) we get later after the discharge from the hospital and that comes after three or four months. Till that time we cannot wait and nobody will wait for that money because there is no scope. We know that nowadays hospitalization means the amount spend is more than ten to twenty thousand rupees. In our case the hospitalization expenditure went sixty to seventy thousand rupees. My brother sold his auto and took some money on loan in order to pay for my treatment. The interest rate is ten per cent and still we are paying that debt. We got five thousand rupees of our 'bima' (medical insurance) but what is the point of it after we take the loan or sell our livelihoods assets. Moreover they just give five thousand rupees which is very negligible amount in comparison to this huge hospital expenditure. The amount is not even enough to

pay interest rate. So you think does it really help us? (Ashok, Pune, 2010).

Even if we get five thousand rupees from the 'aroygya bima policy' (health policy) but we have to pay double. This money goes only in paying the interest rate. They are not paying the amount at the time of illness. So the amount we get is actually not benefitting us (Kamal, Pune, 2010).

Union did this struggle only for us. This health bima is better than nothing. However at times of illness we only have to pay the hospital expenditure by taking loan that becomes a huge burden for us (Seeta, Pune, 2011).

These narratives raise many issues regarding the medical insurance scheme and also express the feelings and experiences of waste pickers about this scheme. Firstly, the sum assured is very less and does not reduce the economic burden. Secondly, it is a reimbursement model and not a cashless model, where the waste picker gets the refund only after 3-4 months which is quite a long period in the context of poor economic conditions of the waste pickers.

When asked about the illnesses which are not covered under this scheme, the waste pickers expressed their disappointment that maternity benefits, HIV/AIDS and cancer are not included. They also mentioned that they were aware only of these diseases being excluded but have no idea about others that may not be covered. They feel that these conditions should be included in the scheme, although they have no knowledge about HIV/AIDS and cancer.

Knowledge and Experience Regarding the Claim Process

The waste pickers from whom information was gathered were aware about the claim procedure they have to follow to get the benefit from medical insurance scheme. The first thing they knew was that they have to inform to the union about any hospitalisation directly or over the phone. They also knew the detail documentation that is required to be submitted while claiming the benefit. According to the waste pickers, they have to claim it within seven days after discharge from the hospital.

However, some waste pickers found the procedures for claim and arranging documents to be lengthy and cumbersome. Many a times, pharmacists (medical store) do not give bills if the bill amount is small. It also happens that in the whole procedure of illness at hospital, they tend to lose the bills because of the stress during hospitalisation. Later it becomes a major hindrance in arranging documents for medical insurance claim.

The waste pickers principally talked about their expectations from this kind of medical insurance scheme and they think that insurance scheme should follow the cashless model instead of the reimbursement model by paying directly to the hospital for the services used. They also felt that the sum assured should be increased and at least should pay half of the amount incurred on hospital expenditure, which will reduce their economic burden considerably.

Major Issues

The workers' experiences show that the union on their part had made great efforts to reduce the economic burden due to health expenditures. However it does not completely ease out the economic burden. It is evident that poor access to public health services compels the waste pickers to avail services from private health facilities which are expensive leading to increased indebtedness. This has meant that even though workers have insurance, they still get indebted due to medical expenses. The insurance scheme's exclusion criteria for outpatient and maternity care, in a context where most of the waste pickers are women and the burden of minor ailments is high, only partially serves the felt needs of the workers. Thus all the medical needs of the workers are not met. It therefore highlights the fact that insurance schemes tend to provide only partial coverage instead of comprehensive health care. The workers themselves have felt that if there would have been cashless model of insurance scheme and if the benefit amount has increased, then it would reduce the economic burden considerably.

Who is Benefiting?

This particular medical insurance scheme which is seen as one of the social security measures is mere tokenism to the worker as only ₹0.5-0.6 million is paid as an annual premium by the PMC. On the other hand, people are forced to go to the private sector due to inefficient public sector which in a way raises serious concern that: are insurance schemes actually a process by which the private sector is being strengthened? Because in this particular medical insurance scheme, even though public subsidy has been given, the money does not go back to the public sector, rather it goes in the hands of private sector.

References

Acharya, S. (2010). "Access to Health Care and Patterns of Discrimination: A Study of Dalit Children in Selected Villages of Gujarat and Rajasthan", *Indian Institute of Dalit Studies, Working Paper Series* 1(2): 1-37.

Ahmed, S. (2007). *Kagad Kach Patra Kashtkari Panchayat (Waste Pickers' Union) Health Insurance Scheme: Case Study.* Institute of Financial Management and Research, Centre for Insurance and Risk Management.

Baraik, V.K. and P.M. Kulkarni (2006). "Health Status and Access to Health Care Services: Disparities among Social Groups in India", *Working Paper Series* I(4): 1-44. Indian Institute of Dalit Studies.

Baru, R. (1999). "The Structure and Utilisation of Health Services: An Intersate Analysis", in M. Rao (ed.), *Disinvesting in Health: World Bank Prescriptions for Health.* New Delhi: Sage Publications. pp.129-44.

Baru, R., A. Acharya, S. Acharya, A. Shiva Kumar and K. Nagaraj (2010). "Inequities in Access to Health Services in India: Caste, Class and Region", *Economic and Political Weekly* XLV(38): 49-57.

Breman, J. (2010). *Outcaste Labour in Asia: Circulation and Informalization of Workforce—The Bottom of the Economy.* New Delhi: Oxford University Press.

Carrin, G., M. Waelkens and B. Criel (2005). "Community-based Health Insurance in Developing Countries: A Study of its Contribution to the Performance of Health Financing Systems", *Tropical Medicine and International Health* 10(8): 799-811.

Chikarmane, P. and L. Narayan (2000). "Formalising Livelihood: Case of Waste-Pickers in Pune", *Economic and Political Weekly* 35(41): 3639-42.

———. (2005). *Case Study on Kagad Kach Patra Kashtakari Panchayat* (Trade Union of Waste Pickers). Available on *http://www.wiego.org/program_areas/org_rep/case-kkpkp.pdf* (accessed on 4 November 2011).

———. (2009). *Rising from the Waste: Organizing Waste Pickers in India, Thailand and the Philippines.* Thailand: Committee for Asian Women (CAW).

Cointreau, S. (2006). *Occupational and Environmental Health Issues of Solid Waste Management: Special Emphasis on Middle- and Lower-Income Countries.* Urban Papers. Washington, D.C.: The World Bank Group and Urban Sector Board.

Devadasan, N., K. Ranson, W. Damme and B. Criel (2004). "Community Health Insurance in India: An Overview", *Economic and Political Weekly* 39(28): 3179-83.

Develtere, P. and Patrick Van Durme (1999-2000). "Social Exclusion, the Informal Sector and Social Economy", *Courier ACP-EU* No.178, December-January. pp.68-70.

Dilip, T. (2005). "Extent of Inequity in Access to Health Care Services in India", in L. Gangooli, R. Duggal and A. Shukla (eds.), *Review of Health Care in India.* Mumbai: Cehat. pp.247-68.

Duggal, R. (2005). "Public Health Expenditures, Investment and Financing Under the Shadow of a Growing Private Sector", in L. Gangooli, R. Duggal and A. Shukla (eds.), *Review of Health Care in India.* Mumbai: Cehat. pp.225-46.

Ellis, R., M. Alam and I. Gupta (2000). "Health Insurance in India Prognosis and Prospects", *Economic and Political Weekly* 35(4): 207-17.

Gilson, L., J. Doherty, R. Loewenson and V. Francis (2007). *Challenging Inequity through Health Systems.* Final Report. Knowledge Network on Health Systems, WHO Commission on the Social Determinants of Health.

Government of India (2002a). *National Health Policy: 2002.* New Delhi: Department of Health, Ministry of Health and Family Welfare.

———. (2002b). *The Second National Labour Commission Report.* New Delhi: Ministry of Labour. Available on *http://labour.nic.in* (accessed on 23 October 2010).

Gumber, A. and V. Kulkarni (2000). "Health Insurance for Informal Sector: Case Study of Gujarat", *Economic and Political Weekly* 35(40): 3607-13.

Hart, T.J. (2000). "Commentary-Three Decades of the Inverse Care Law", *British Medical Journal* 320(7226): 18-19.

Hayami, Y., A. Dikshit and S. Mishra (2003). "Waste Pickers and Collectors in Delhi: Poverty and Environment in an Urban Informal Sector", *Discussion Paper on International Development Strategies* No. 2003-004. Foundation for Advanced Studies on International Development and Society for Economic and Social Research.

Holmstrom, M. (1985). *Industry and Inequality: The Social Anthropology of Indian Labour.* Cambridge: Cambridge University Press.

Hunt, C. (1996). "Child Waste Pickers in India: The Occupational and its Health Risks", *Environment and Urbanization* 8(2): 111-18.

International Institute for Population Sciences (IIPS) and Macro International (2007). *National Family Health Survey (NFHS-3), 2005-06, India: Key Findings.* Mumbai: IIPS.

Krishnan, T. (1999). "Access To Health and The Burden of Treatment in India: An Inter State Comparison", in M. Rao (ed.), *Disinvesting in Health: The World Bank Prescriptions For Health.* New Delhi: Sage Publications. pp.212-30.

Kuria, D. and R. Muasya (2010). *Mapping of Waste Pickers and Organizations Supporting Waste Pickers in Kenya.* Commissioned by Women in Informal Employment: Globalizing and Organizing (WIEGO). Available on *http://www.inclusivecities.org/pdfs/Kenya%20Mappingweb.pdf* (accessed on 15 May 2011).

Mavalankar, D. and R. Bhat (2000). *Health Insurance in India: Opportunities, Challenges and Concerns.* Ahmedabad: Indian Institute of Management.

Medina, M. (2005). *Waste Picker Cooperatives in Developing Countries*, Paper prepared for WIEGO/ Cornell/SEWA Conference on Membership-Based Organizations of the Poor. Ahmedabad.

National Commission for Enterprises in the Unorganised Sector (2007). *Report on Conditions of Work and Promotion of livelihoods in the Unorganised Sector.* New Delhi.

———. (2009). *The Challenge of Employment in India: An Informal Economy Perspective*. New Delhi: Academic Foundation.

Nguyen, H., G. Chalin, M. Lam and W. Maclaren (2003). *Health and Social Needs of Waste Pickers in Vietnam*. Research Paper. Canadian International Development Agency (CIDA), Waste-ECON Programme, South East Asia. Available on *http://www.utoronto.ca/waste-econ /Huyen Nguyen.pdf* (accessed on 3 March 2011).

NSSO (2006). *Morbidity, Health Care and the Condition of the Aged, National Sample Survey*, 60th Round (January-June 2004). Report No 507. New Delhi: Ministry of Statistics and Programme Implementation, Government of India.

Qadeer, I. and D. Roy (1989). "Work, Wealth and Health: Sociology of Workers' Health in India", *Social Scientist* 17(5/6): 45-92.

Ranson, M. (2002). "Reduction of Catastrophic Health Care Expenditures by a Community-based Health Insurance Scheme in Gujarat, India: Current Experiences and Challenges", *Bulletin of the World Health Organization* 80: 613-21.

Rao, S. (2005). "Health Insurance in India", Background paper in *Financing and Delivery of Health Care Services in India*. New Delhi: National Commission on Macroeconomics and Health MHFW, Government of India. pp.275-292.

Samson, M. (2009). *Refusing to be Cast Aside: Waste Pickers Organizing around the World*. Cambridge MA, USA: Women in Informal Employment: Globalizing and Organizing (WIEGO).

Sarkar, P. (2003). "Solid Waste Management in Delhi: A Social Vulnerability Study", in Martin J. Bunch, V. Madha Suresh and T. Vasantha Kumaran (eds.), *Proceedings of the Third International Conference on Environment and Health*. Chennai, India.

Scott, K. (2010). *The Current State of Health Insurance Coverage in India: Current Schemes and Future Prospects*. Paper prepared for SATHI, Pune.

Sen, G., A. Iyer and A. George (2007). "Systematic Hierarchies and Systematic Failures", *Economic and Political Weekly* 42(8): 682-90.

SNDT Women's University and Chintan Environmental Research and Action Group (2008). *Recycling Livelihoods: Integration of the Informal Recycling Sector in Solid Waste Management in India*. Available at *http://www 2.gtz.de/dokumente/bib-2010/gtz2010-0485en-informal-recyclingindia.pdf* (accessed on 2 February 2011).

Tamara, Failor (2010). "Improving Services and Improving Lives: Waste-Picker Integration and Municipal Coproduction in Pune, India", *Carolina Papers on International Development* No. 25, Fall. UNC Global, Chapel Hill.

Thorat, S. and N. Sabharwal (2010). "Caste and Social Exclusion: Issues Related to Concept, Indicators and Measurement", *Children, Social Exclusion and Development: Working Paper Series* 2(1): 1-34. Indian Institute of Dalit Studies and UNICEF.

Wilson, D., V. Costas and C. Cheeseman (2006). "Role of Informal Sector Recycling in Waste Management in Developing Countries", *Habitat International* 30: 797-808.

4

N. PURENDRA PRASAD

State, Community Health Insurance and Commodification of Health Care

A Case of Arogyasri in Andhra Pradesh[1]

Medical neo-liberalism is characterised by commodification of health that transforms individuals from patients to consumers. Unlike patients, consumers who seek health care bear the responsibility for the choices they make or fail to make regarding their health. As consumers are positioned to make choices about health care, they also have the obligation to utilise whatever products and services are available to ensure health or to treat illness and disease. Thus, Fisher (2007) points out that patients as consumers have embraced the neo-liberal logics of health care so that they too see illness in reductionist terms and seek pharmaceuticals as targeted magic bullets. With the growing tailor-made products and medical cost, access and affordability to health care has become a key issue across the world.

In the Indian context, the increased disease burden on the poor along with rapidly growing health care costs has been the subject of debate for some time now. The 9th edition of *National Health Profile 2013* indicated that per capita private expenditure on health is 3-4 times higher than per capita public expenditure in all major states except some northeastern states and Jammu & Kashmir (J&K) (The Hindu, 2014). Services in government health care institutions have declined over the past two decades at the primary and secondary level, leaving the sick-poor with no option but to seek private health care services. Several studies have pointed out that rising expenditure

---

1. This is a revised version of the paper "Health Care Models in the Era of Medical Neo-liberalism" published in *Economic and Political Weekly*, in 2012.

on health and education is one of the main contributory factors to high indebtedness and subsequent suicides among peasants in different parts of the country in the last 10 years (Sarma, 2004; Ghosh, 2006).

Clearly, health care has assumed a huge political significance for the neo-liberal state. New and innovative (populist) health care programmes are being conceived in several states in different forms. Among these, Rajiv Arogyasri, a community health insurance scheme introduced by the Government of Andhra Pradesh (GoAP), on pilot basis in the year 2007 and implemented in the year 2008, is hailed by many experts as a model to be emulated. The scheme covers 1.83 lakh BPL (below poverty line) families.

Arogyasri in Andhra Pradesh (AP) needs special attention as it is supposed to have mobilised large number of voters for the ruling Congress party and is credited with bringing Congress party to power second time in the year 2009. This scheme's popularity is so huge that several delegations from different states in India have been regularly studying the logic of it so that it can be replicated in order to reap similar political benefits. States such as Kerala, Tamil Nadu, Delhi and Karnataka have already formulated a similar template and are in the process of implementing it. Government of Maharashtra announced Rajiv Gandhi Jeevandayee Arogya Yojana, a free medicare scheme for the poor in the year 2011. The government of Maharashtra committed ₹8,000 million which is supposed to benefit nearly 5 million families in eight districts in the first phase for families earning below ₹0.1 million per annum. A national social health insurance scheme called Rashtriya Swashthya Bima Yojana (RSBY) was launched as a centrally sponsored scheme (CSS) in 2008 covering 23 million families and 70 million beneficiaries. GoAP has already announced that Arogyasri will soon be converted into a universal health scheme extending its scope to non-BPL families as well. Given the pre-eminence of the scheme, it is important for us to arrive at a careful assessment of the scheme by locating it in the historical evolution of health care systems in India and the underlying socio-economic and political dynamics in this chapter.

I

Political Economy of Health

The recommendations of Sir John Bhore Committee in 1946 had a tremendous impact on the health care model adopted in the post-independent India. The committee recognised the existing inequalities and recommended that no individual should fail to secure adequate medical care because of inability to pay for it. On that basis, it recommended that medical services should be free for all without any discrimination and discussed the dire consequences of privatisation of health care and urban bias that prevailed in health sector (Bhore Committee Report, 1946).

Although the class interests of India's new rulers came to the fore after Independence, the Nehruvian state adopted a liberal stance given the democratic urge kindled among the masses in the wake of freedom from colonial rule. This impelled the ruling classes to take such actions in health and other fields in the first two decades after Independence that placed India high among the newly independent countries. As a result, protection and promotion of health and nutrition of the people were placed in the Directive Principles of State Policy in the Constitution of India. This phase is labelled the "golden two decades of public health in India" (Banerji, 2001: 44).

The major achievements during this period include the mass BCG campaign of the 1950s, the 1958-1963 National Malaria Eradication Programme, the setting up of National Tuberculosis Institute and National Institute of Health Administration and Education to train physicians to inculcate managerial, epidemiological, social and political capabilities, the establishment of PHCs (primary health centres), the minimum needs programme, the multipurpose workers' scheme, the CHWs (community health workers)-VHG (village health guide) scheme, and the National Health Policy.

However, the political vision to establish a comprehensive health care service system was unfortunately short lived; over the next three decades, there was a sharp decline in the quality of health services in the country. The year 1967 marked the beginning of a steep decline in health services, culminating in the present state of its serious 'sickness'. The major factors that contributed to this decline were: (a) obsessive pre-occupation with the family planning programme at the cost of serious neglect of health service needs of the poor; (b) imposition of the so-called international initiatives in health; and (c) considerable involvement of the western powers in shaping social (including health), economic and political policies of the country in the form of pressures for privatisation through the structural adjustment programme (SAP) from the late 1980s onwards (Banerji, 2001: 45).

India was a signatory to the Alma-Ata declaration in 1978 as a member country of the World Health Organization (WHO), which tried to reinforce the principles of sharing power, the distribution of resources, etc. However, the idea of 'selective primary health care'[2] negated the spirit of this declaration. This led the very same WHO and United Nations Children's Fund (UNICEF) to make a U-turn in advocating the implementation of specific vertical programmes such as the universal programme for immunisation, oral rehydration and other child survival strategies and social marketing of contraceptives. Considerable damage was inflicted upon the provision of comprehensive health services by according overriding priority to a single vertical programme over the former. Despite the considerable weaknesses of these programmes in terms of their economic, administrative and epidemiological sustainability in India, the western powers pushed it for political and ideological reasons. Thus, these programmes paved the way for the growth of private health care in India (Banerji, 2001: 46), marginalised other medical systems, and the mandate of a welfare state in terms of health and education provisions was diluted gradually.

The private health sector grew consistently because of the exemption of import duty for expensive medical equipment, subsidised rates for land to build hospitals, reimbursement provision for all government employees to avail health services in corporate hospitals, etc. Besides the numerous concessions given by the

2. Andhra Pradesh is referred to here as 'undivided' state prior to 2 June 2014. Even after bifurcation of the state into Telangana and Andhra Pradesh, the community health insurance scheme Arogyasri is continued by both the state governments.

government to the private health care sector in the late 1970s and early 1980s, privatisation of health care received a further boost due to global recession, which imposed fiscal constraints on government budgets and encouraged them to cut back on public expenditure in the social sector (Baru, 1998).

As Zachariah *et al.* (2010: 24) pointed out, the government completely divested its responsibility for curative health care as well. This led to the unfettered growth of hospitals that found it lucrative to adopt the tertiary care model. With good quality health services becoming unaffordable and inaccessible, curative health care today is left to the initiative of the patient. Also, the private sector grew without any controls by using investments made by the state (Baru, 2003), thus triggring the first wave of privatisation during the 1980s. With growth of the pharmaceutical and medical equipment industries in the post-1990s, the second wave of privatisation, i.e., corporatisation of health care, became firmly entrenched in India. These national health policies are reflected in governance mechanisms in different states with some regional variations.

II

Structure of Health Services in Andhra Pradesh

In AP's government health sector, there were 1,570 PHCs, 12,522 sub-centres and 164 community health centres (CHCs) with 3,047 doctors[3] serving around 60 million people in the rural areas in 2009. In brief, there were four hospitals[4] and 3 dispensaries per 1 million people, and 45 beds and 10 doctors per 0.1 million people. These statistics reveal the inadequate health infrastructure and health providers in the government health sector in AP. According to the WHO guidelines (*Human Development Report* [HDR], 2007), there is a need for at least another 500 PHCs and 400 CHCs in the state to provide basic health services. However instead of strengthening the

3. Selective primary health care was conceived and funded by Rockfeller Foundation and Ford Foundation.

4. There are a total of 7,721 doctors and 494 contract doctors in both urban (general and specialist hospitals) and rural India (sub-centres, PHCs, CHCs).

public health sector, the state government accelerated the growth of private health care providers through economic reforms.

One of the other reasons for the growth of private medical health care in the state was the availability of surplus agricultural income. By late 1960s and early 1970s, a stratum of agriculturists (landowning castes such as Kammas, Kapus, Reddys and Velamas) were looking at new avenues for investing their savings/profits accumulated from intensive farming of paddy and high-value cash crops such as Virginia tobacco, turmeric, chillies, etc. In other words, with a new class of investors emerging in AP, its economy reached a phase where the rich peasantry and regional bourgeoisie together worked for the creation of better conditions for economic growth (Upadhya, 1997) and started influencing government policies to suit their business interests in various sectors, including the health industry.

During the late 1970s and early 1980s, many of these land-owning castes started establishing corporate hospitals. For example, Pratap C. Reddy established his first Apollo Hospital in Chennai in 1983 and K. Sambasiva Rao, a Kamma from Krishna District, established Medwin Hospitals in Hyderabad. At present, the Apollo Hospitals group owns and manages 38 hospitals, making it Asia's largest and the world's fourth largest health care provider. Yashoda Hospital, Reddy Laboratories and other pharmaceutical companies established hospitals during the 1970s and 1980s (Damodaran, 2008: 109-16). With the beginning of economic reforms in the 1990s, AP witnessed a high spurt of private health care institutions and pharmaceutical companies.

A survey by the state government in 1994 showed that private hospitals accounted for 59 per cent of the total hospitals in the state with 35 per cent in the public sector and 6 per cent in the voluntary sector (GoAP, 1993-94) resulting in higher health expenditure and out-of-pocket (OOP) expenses for different categories of people. According to the National Sample Survey (NSS) 61st (2004-05) round, on an average nearly 6 per cent of total household consumption expenditure is spent on medical care (both institutional and non-institutional) in AP, which is higher than the all-India average of 4.7 per cent (HDR, 2007).

During 1990-91, there were 184 private nursing homes and hospitals in Hyderabad-Secunderabad; of which 166 were managed by single owners or partners, 11 were specialist nursing homes and 7 were managed as private and public-limited enterprises. By 1997, the number of private nursing homes and hospitals had risen from 184 to 400 (Narayana, 2003: 102). A survey conducted in 2004 of private hospitals with 100 or more beds in Hyderabad found that there were 28 hospitals with a total of 5,495 beds. Among them, 16 were corporate hospitals accounting for 57 per cent of the beds. By 2004, the number of corporate hospitals in Hyderabad city alone increased to 16 with a total bed-strength of 2,981. While most corporate hospitals were newly established, a few existing private hospitals were upgraded. There were 10 trust hospitals, which accounted for 35 per cent of the hospital beds. A large number of corporate hospitals had come into existence in Hyderabad and other cities in the state after 2004 (Narayana, 2009). According to the Andhra Pradesh Private Hospitals and Nursing Homes Association (APNA), there were 857 private hospitals in Hyderabad alone in 2010.

Health Reforms in the 1980s

N.T. Rama Rao, Chief Minister of the state in the early 1980s, introduced two major health reforms during his tenure. One was the establishment of Andhra Pradesh Vaidya Vidhan Parishad (APVVP), an independent body, in 1986 to implement health services at the secondary level. The second was the Nizam Institute of Medical Sciences (NIMS),[5] a tertiary hospital in Hyderabad, which was restructured such that it had to raise its own revenues from paying patients while the government provided grants only for its infrastructure. While APVVP introduced more complexity and opaqueness into the health governance structure, the NIMS model created a hierarchy among paying and non-paying patients in the government hospitals. In order to strengthen APVVP and pursue reforms, the state government implemented the first health referral

5. There were 349 general hospitals (with 36,168 beds) and 262 dispensaries with 7,415 doctors (including contract doctors) to serve the 80 million population of AP.

project in 1995 with the help of a World Bank loan of ₹6,080 million. This inaugurated health reforms in the state as a part of the SAP in the state.

These reforms resulted in gradual withdrawal of the state and paved the way for hiring of more contract workers in public health and sanitation,[6] negligence towards health infrastructure in government hospitals, etc. The state government issued a government order (GO) in 2006 to hand over a PHC to a private NGO (non-governmental organisation) in Anantapur district. Later, attempts were made to hand over PHCs to NGOs in Gadeguda and Lingapur in Adilabad district. In the name of pilot projects, the state government selected at least 36 PHCs in order to privatise them. As part of the reforms process, the state government established hospital development societies, issued GOs to collect user charges and handed over the urban health posts (now renamed as urban health centres) in all cities and towns to private organisations.

The overall decline in the health budget, particularly after introduction of the SAP, has further worsened the situation, leading to the scarcity of resources in the health sector. The share of the health sector in the state budget was the highest (6.5%) in the Fifth Five Year Plan period. Thereafter, it declined continuously and fell to 5.2 per cent in the Eighth Plan, 4.5 per cent by 2005-06 in the Tenth Plan and 3.6 per cent in the Eleventh Plan period. The proportion of public expenditure on the health sector to state domestic product (SDP) declined from 1.29 per cent in the Seventh Plan to 0.94 per cent in the Eighth Plan. Thus, after SAP, there was a considerable decline in the allocation of resources to health services in the government sector (HDR, 2007: 90-91).

Not surprisingly, the state's performance has lagged among the 15 major Indian states according to the *National Human Development Report 2001*. While the state was ranked 9th in 1991, it slipped down to the 10th spot in 2001. The better performing states were Kerala,

---

6. NIMS is a hospital given on a 99-year lease to the state government by the Nizam Charitable Trust in 1976.

Tamil Nadu, Punjab and Maharashtra.[7] Average life expectancy in AP according to the 2001 Census is 62 years, which is below the national average of 64.6 years.[8] The gradual decline of the public health sector and the rapid growth of the private and corporate health sector from the mid-1980s provide the context in which new health innovations can be understood.

III

Arogyasri: A New Health Care Model or Populism?

According to the state government:

> Rural population of state, majority of whom are farmers, are not having access to advanced medical treatments and are silent sufferers of ill-health. This is true in case of diseases related to heart, kidney, brain, cancer and injuries due to domestic accidents and burns. While the Government is in the process of adequately strengthening the health institutions for basic health care, lack of specialist doctors and equipment for treatment of serious diseases has created a wide gap between the disease load and the capacity of the Government hospitals to serve the poor. These facilities though available in corporate sector are catering mainly to the affordable sections of society and are beyond the reach of poor families living in villages. Because of this gap poor patients are constrained to go to private hospitals for treatment and in the process incur huge debts leading to sale of properties and assets or are, sometimes, left eventually to die.[9]

This is the justification for introducing Arogyasri to assist the BPL families for treating dreaded diseases. In order to facilitate effective implementation of the scheme, the government set up the Arogyasri Health Care Trust under chairmanship of the chief minister. The trust, in consultation with specialists in the field of insurance and

---

7. On an average, 60-70 per cent of the workers in municipalities including Greater Hyderabad Municipal Corporation (GHMC) are contract workers while in some urban local bodies such as Visakhapatnam, the contract workers account for 80 per cent of the total workforce (Prasad, 2014).

8. *National Human Development Report 2001*, Planning Commission of India, Government of India (GoI).

9. Registrar General of India, NFHS III 2005-06 Fact Sheets.

medical professionals, devised a tailor-made insurance scheme. The insurance premium works out to about ₹250 per family unit. The total reimbursement of ₹0.15 million can be availed either by an individual or for the entire family. An additional sum of ₹50,000 is provided as a buffer to take care of expenses if costs exceed the original allocation. As an exception, the cost for cochlear implant surgery with auditory verbal therapy is reimbursed by the Arogyasri Trust up to a maximum of ₹0.65 million for each patient.

The Arogyasri Trust has empanelled 491 hospitals in the state, of which nearly 80 per cent are in the private sector while the remaining 20 per cent are government hospitals. Although the Arogyasri scheme is meant for poor villagers, there is not even one private hospital in the rural areas, while the distribution of empanelled government hospitals in rural and urban areas is almost even (Table 4.1). Going by the Arogyasri Trust data, the government health sector is in a better position to serve the rural BPL population compared to the private health sector. However instead of strengthening government hospitals and routing the Arogyasri scheme through this rural and urban hospital network, why have private and corporate hospitals received privileged treatment is a question that few studies have raised (Shukla *et al.*, 2011). A similar question—whether Arogyasri has the potential to reduce financial burden on the BPL population and improve the health of sick-poor—has also been raised (Mitchell *et al.*, 2011).

Inclusion of Diseases

Official documents describe Arogyasri as a unique public-private partnership (PPP) model in the field of health insurance that is customised to meet the health needs of poor patients and provide end-to-end cashless services for identified diseases through a network of service providers from private and government sectors.[10] In 2007, when Arogyasri was launched, 163 procedures were identified for reimbursement but with growing popularity of the scheme and demand, the list of procedures that was eligible for reimbursement

10. *http//www.Arogyasri.org*, accessed on 5 January 2010.

increased to about 938 in 2011. An analysis of this list of diseases indicates that of the 938 procedures, Star Health and Allied Insurance companies manage the reimbursement for 352 procedures while the Arogyasri Trust manages the remaining 586.

Table 4.1

List of Government and Private Hospitals Empanelled by Arogyasri Trust

		Government Hospitals		*Private Hospitals*	
No.	*District Name*	*Rural*	*Urban*	*Rural*	*Urban*
1	Hyderabad	-----	14	-----	111
2	East Godavari	02	02	0	32
3	West Godavari	05	01	0	16
4	Krishna	03	03	0	29
5	Warangal	01	04	0	19
6	Guntur	02	02	0	30
7	Anantpur	02	01	0	07
8	YSR	01	0	0	03
9	Nalgonda	06	02	0	01
10	Karimnagar	01	03	0	19
11	Adilabad	01	01	0	03
12	Nizamabad	03	01	0	03
13	Chittor	04	02	0	12
14	Vizianagaram	01	01	0	06
15	Srikakulam	01	01	0	04
16	Ranga Reddy	0	01	0	01
17	Medak	02	03	0	01
18	Mahboobnagar	02	02	0	09
19	Vishakapatnam	02	02	0	33
20	Kurnool	02	03	0	14
21	Nellore	04	01	0	12
22	Khammam	02	01	0	08
23	Prakasham	02	02	0	16
	Total	49	53	0	389

Source: Data extracted from the official website of Arogyasri Trust, 10 December 2011.

At the time of the scheme's inception, the government agreed to pay a premium of ₹338 towards each BPL family to the insurance company. But with the increased financial burden, the government renegotiated a reduced rate of ₹217 annual premium with the insurance company. Our interaction with the corporate hospitals indicated a series of complaints about reimbursements from government sources, especially inordinate delays unlike the insurance companies which release the reimbursement money immediately. However, even with this reduced rate of ₹217, private hospitals earn significantly because of the increased number of procedures from 163 to 938. The procedures approved are often high-cost interventions and the difference in the cost of the procedure determined in 2008 and the current cost still fetches private hospitals substantial profits due to the increased patient base (Shukla *et al.*, 2011: 40).

Indeed, beginning with Emergency Medical Relief Insurance (EMRI), along with the ambulance services (108 and 104), followed by Rajiv Arogyasri, later free dialysis machines, currently all laboratory and diagnostic services in government hospitals are to be managed by the private companies. Implemented through the PPP model, these schemes rely on non-state entities to deliver health care to the poor. During our interviews, government health officials cited poor infrastructure, lack of planning, and inefficient use of health care staff in government hospitals as some of the reasons to justify PPP projects. They also indicated that Arogyasri scheme has been providing assured clientele and financial incentives that has contributed to the steady growth of medium and large private hospitals.

Centralisation of Health Services

The government provided Arogyasri health card to BPL families. These cardholders are told that they have freedom to avail the surgical facility in any hospital across the state. This 'freedom' will entail the patient to avail the best quality techno-commercial treatment in the specialty and super-specialty corporate hospitals. This is one mechanism by which super specialty hospitals located in urban centres gained access to the sick-poor across the state.

Moreover, the insurance company and private health sector have devised direct control over scrutiny and case referral of patients through Arogyamitras, a cadre of private health workers who are located in PHCs, CHCs and district/state hospitals to facilitate the BPL patients from rural to urban hospitals. It has been pointed out that Arogyamitras function as a parallel administration. It is these people who help divert cases from the government to private hospitals (Shukla *et al.*, 2011: 39).

Through Arogyasri and Arogya Yojanas, 'new choices' are being created for sick-poor within the medical neo-liberal discourse. However discussion with a few doctors in Osmania hospital indicated that these are not new choices but rather new ways of invoking surgical interventions without adequate rationale. Indeed, access to surgery-based intervention is perceived by the sick-poor as a natural choice in the situation they find themselves. Certainly, several of these poor individuals who otherwise would not have got access to expensive technological medicine, certainly felt greatly satisfied. Thus, health has not been a choice but an imposed preference for a large majority of the population (Prasad, 2007).

Since inception, there were 14,18,489 surgeries registered under Arogyasri as on 7 December 2011. The data indicate that 35 per cent of surgeries were done in Hyderabad alone, another 34 per cent in 4 major hospital network cities (Vijayawada, Visakhapatnam, Guntur and Kakinada) and another 24 per cent in 6 medium urban centres (Nellore, Warangal, Chittor, Karimnagar, Kurnool and Rajmundry). Thus, 93 per cent of the surgeries were done in 11 cities where private and corporate hospital network is well established, while 7 per cent surgeries in the remaining 12 districts with poor health infrastructure (see Table 4.2).

The data also indicate that of 14,18,489 surgeries conducted till date in the entire state, 83 per cent were performed in private sector hospitals and only 17 per cent in government hospitals. When we look at the district-wise distribution of surgeries conducted, 90 per cent and more surgeries till date were conducted in private/corporate hospitals in 17 of the 23 districts in the state; in the remaining six districts, the government hospitals' share in these surgeries was about 25 per cent, while 75 per cent of surgeries were conducted in private hospitals (see Table 4.3). This is a clear indication of how Arogyasri has helped in the growth of private and corporate health sector in the state.

Table 4.2

District-wise Total Number of Surgeries under Arogyasri

S.No.	*District Name*	*No. of Surgeries*	*%*
1	Hyderabad	5,01,206	35.3
2	Adilabad	1516	0.10
3	Anantpur	13,344	0.94
4	Chittor	60,307	4.25
5	East Godavari	1,03,940	7.32
6	Guntur	1,23,762	8.72
7	YSR	6718	0.47
8	Khammam	13,232	0.93
9	Kurnool	46,705	3.29
10	Krishna	1,28,259	9.04
11	Karimnagar	46,143	3.25
12	Mahboobnagar	8364	0.58
13	Medak	2100	0.14
14	Nalgonda	6166	0.43
15	Nellore	83,630	5.89
16	Nizamabad	8719	0.61
17	Prakasham	12,493	0.88
18	Ranga Reddy	2384	0.16
29	Srikakulam	8557	0.60
20	Vishakapatnam	1,24,723	8.79
21	Vizianagaram	15,758	1.11
22	Warangal	59,851	4.21
23	West Godavari	40,612	2.86
		14, 18,489	99.87

Source: Data extracted from the official website of Arogyasri Trust, 7 December 2011.

Although the state government directed all government hospitals to utilise the funds under Arogyasri, the latter are struggling to

Table 4.3

District-wise Total Number of Surgeries in Government and Private Hospitals

		No. of Surgeries in Hospitals		
S.No.	District Name	Government	Private	Total
1	Hyderabad	1,22,624 (24.46%)	3,78,582 (75.53%)	5,01,206 (99.99%)
2	Adilabad	134 (8.83%)	1,382 (91.16%)	1,516 (99.99%)
3	Anantpur	1,803 13.51%)	11,541 (86.48%)	13,344 (99.99%)
4	Chittor	1,641 (2.72%)	58,666 (97.27%)	60,307 (99.99%)
5	East Godavari	31,068 (29.89%)	72,872 (70.1%)	1,03,940 (99.99%)
6	Guntur	31,047 (25.08%)	92,715 (74.91%)	1,23,762 (99.99%)
7	YSR	0 (0%)	6,718 (100%)	6,718 (100%)
8	Khammam	347 (2.62%)	12,885 (97.37%)	13,232 (99.99%)
9	Kurnool	17,084 (36.57%)	29,621 (63.42%)	46,705 (99.99%)
10	Krishna	7,941 (6.19%)	1,20,318 (93.80%)	1,28,259 (99.99%)
11	Karimnagar	629 (1.36%)	45,514 (98.63)	46,143 (99.99%)
12	Mahboobnagar	802 (9.58%)	7,562 (90.41%)	8,364 (99.99%)
13	Medak	422 (20.09%)	1,678 (79.9%)	2,100 (99.99%)
14	Nalgonda	2,176 (35.29%)	3,990 (64.7%)	6,166 (99.99%)
15	Nellore	729 (0.87%)	82,901 (99.12%)	83,630 (99.99%)
16	Nizamabad	1,125 (12.9%)	7,594 (87.09%)	8,719 (99.99%)
17	Prakasham	823 (6.58%)	11,670 (93.41%)	12,493 (99.99%)
18	Ranga Reddy	0 (0%)	2,384 (100%)	2,384 (100%)
29	Srikakulam	42 (0.49%)	8,515 (99.50%)	8,557 (99.99%)
20	Vishakapatnam	3,727 (2.98%)	1,20,996 (97.01%)	1,24,723 (99.99%)
21	Vizianagaram	1469 (9.32%)	14,289 (90.67%)	15,758 (99.99%)
22	Warangal	12,877 (21.51%)	46,974 (78.48%)	59,851 (99.99%)
23	West Godavari	1,445 (3.55%)	39,167 (96.44%)	40,612 (99.99%)
	Total	2,39,955 (16.91%)	11,78,534 (83.08%)	14,18,489 (99.99%)

Note: Figures in brackets are in percentages.

Source: Data extracted from the official website of Arogyasri Trust, 7 December 2011.

compete with the super-specialty corporate and private hospitals. However, the specialty hospitals in government sector are able to utilise the resources allotted to them. For instance, Gandhi Hospital, a 1200-bed government hospital with annual budget of ₹120 million, performed 25,893 operations in 2006. On the other hand, the total number of surgeries conducted by private hospitals under Arogyasri was 59,846 by August 2008 and the amount paid to them was ₹2,252 million (Raja Reddy, 2008: 21). Indeed, of the per capita value from Arogyasri funds received by different hospitals, corporate hospitals obtained a higher value compared to government hospitals despite the fact that the latter serves a large proportion of patients under this scheme. Estimates indicate that the per capita value of Arogyasri in Osmania General Hospital is ₹12,298; in NIMS, an autonomous government hospital, it is ₹36,291, while in Care Banjara, a corporate hospital, it is ₹78,808 (Vijay, 2012).

Several reports[11] indicate that corporate hospitals show interest only in surgeries that are financially remunerative and "other cases", which are less remunerative, but high risk cases are referred to government hospitals. For instance, double-stent cardiac cases, double-valve replacement cardiathoracic (CT) surgeries, hemiplegia, tumours in neurosurgery and several such cases are not taken up by private hospitals. Such patients are persuaded by the private hospitals to approach government hospitals. In one such instance, when a patient named Sattemma, aged 35 years from Kondapur village of Anantsagar mandal in Medak district suffering from a tumour, approached a corporate hospital in Hyderabad, the neurosurgeon indicated that the surgery would cost about ₹0.2 million and require longer post-operative care and immediately referred her to Osmania General Hospital.

A critical scrutiny of surgery procedures related to specific diseases undertaken in Hyderabad has been analysed here. Hyderabad is the only city in the state that has a strong presence of specialty and super-specialty government institutions with credibility that can match private and corporate hospitals. So the Hyderabad data provide us several insights into working of the Arogyasri model.

The 938 procedures approved by Arogyasri have been classified under 29 broad medical categories/systems. For the purpose of analysis, we have taken 20 major private hospitals and 11 major government hospitals in Hyderabad that had handled surgeries under 29 medical categories till 10 December 2011 (Table 4.4). The data pertaining to seven medical categories accounting for 1,70,000 cases indicate that private hospitals managed the maximum high cost

11. Arogyasri Brochure, 2010.

surgical intervention cases such as cochlear implant surgery (100%), medical oncology (98%), radiation oncology (98%), surgical oncology (84%), cardiac and cardiothoracic surgery (79%), genitourinary surgeries (78%), and neurosurgery (53%).

Private hospitals with good medical equipment, infrastructure and managerial capabilities are in a strong position to lobby with the state health bureaucracy, negotiate terms with Star Insurance Company favourably and rely on Arogyamitras to divert high-cost surgical cases and rural medical practitioners (RMPs) as agents to refer appropriate cases to them. Special incentives are created for Arogyamitras, RMPs and agents[12] to bring in appropriate cases to private and corporate hospitals. As a result, private hospitals are able to generate substantial profits from Arogyasri cases. Government hospitals such as Osmania General Hospital, Gandhi Hospital and even NIMS lack appropriate technical equipment and therefore are not in a position to handle even one cochlear implant surgery case. Although the state government states that eventually Arogyasri funds will help the development of infrastructure in government hospitals, the scheme has in fact affected the credibility of all these tertiary hospitals in terms of teaching, research and training medical students.

Our interaction with doctors in Osmania and Gandhi Hospitals indicated that corporate hospitals are interested in surgeries that are not only profitable but less risky. For example, the average length of stay for neurology patients must be a minimum of five to seven days of hospitalisation. Private hospitals showed little interest in these cases because of their low-cost reimbursement and risks associated with post-surgical care. Accordingly, 82 per cent of the neurology cases were handled by government hospitals. Similarly, most of the surgeries related to ENT (92%), general medicine (94%), ophthalmology (99.6%), paediatrics (93%), paediatric surgeries (89%), pulmonology (69%), rheumatology (99.5%), etc., costing less than ₹60,000 were carried out by government hospitals (Table 4.4).

12. Chedda Aspathrulu, Andhra Jyothi, 18, 2011 and "Padakesina Prabhuthva Vaidyam", Eenadu, 11 April 2010.

There were instances reported where private hospitals did not admit emergency cases related to critical care, polytrauma etc. and asked the patients to approach government hospitals. Indeed, post-operative care has been one of the grey areas in Arogyasri, where sick-poor are discharged without much post-operative care and any complications arising from it will have to be borne by them.

Table 4.4

Medical Category-wise Surgeries by Private and Government Hospitals in Hyderbad as on 10 December 2011

S.No.	*Name of the Surgery*	*No. of Surgeries in Government Hospitals**	*No. of Surgeries in Private Hospitals***	*Cost of Procedures (in ₹)*
1	Cardiac and Cardiothoracic Surgery	12,398	46,911	15,000 to 1,50,000
2.	Cardiology	4869	4236	20,000 to 95,000
3	Cochlear Implant Surgery	0	728	20,000 to 5,20,000
4	Critical Care	867	420	45,000 to 1,20,000
5	Dermatology	124	41	20,000 to 30,000
6	Endocrinology	244	17	12,000 to 1,00,000
7	ENT Surgery	5459	453	10,000 to 50,000
8	Gastroenterology	1513	124	5,000 to 1,50,000
9	General Medicine	984	64	20,000 to 50,000
10	General Surgery	7921	5696	10,000 to 80,000
11	Genito Urinary Surgeries	5726	20, 846	10,000 to 1,40,000
12	Gynaecology and Obstetrics Surgery	2084	2114	20,000 to 40,000
13	Infectious Diseases	06	0	20,000 to 25,000

contd...

14	Medical Oncology	1746	93, 234	800 to 60,000
15	Nephrology	10383	10780	15,000 to 35,000
16	Neurology	5918	1272	8,000 to 1,00,000
17	Neurosurgery	10468	12283	15,000 to 1,60,000
18	Ophthalmology Surgery	2316	09	3,000 to 65,000
19	Orthopaedic Surgery and Procedures	2664	2138	15,000 to 50,000
20	Paediatric Surgeries	5683	679	10,000 to 60,000
21	Paediatrics	10863	851	25,000 to 90,000
22	Plastic Surgery	3966	971	10,000 to 1,20,000
23	Poly trauma	10116	5500	3,000 to 1,50,000
24	Prostheses	01	0	500 to 6,000
25	Pulmonology	836	373	15,000 to 50,000
26	Radiation Oncology	1120	44595	2500 to 1,00,000
27	Rheumatology	993	05	10,000 to 50,000
28	Surgical Gastroenterology	1567	1019	25,000 to 1,00,000
29	Surgical Oncology	2955	15349	3,000 to I,00,000

Note: *: Government hospitals include: District Hospital King Koti, Gandhi, Maternity-Hyderabad, ENT-Koti, General and Chest Hospital, Mahavir Hospital & Research Centre, Niloufer, Osmania General Hospital, SRRITCD Govt Fever Hospital, MNJ Hospital, Sarojini Devi Eye Hospital and Durga Bhai Deshmukh Hospital.

**: Private hospitals include: Apollo, Image, Kamineni, KIMS, Narayana Hrudalaya, Medicity, Medwin, Quality Care India, Sigma, Yashoda, New Life Hospital, Hyderabad Nursing Home, Innova Childrens Heart Hospital, Owaisi, Aware Global Hospitals, Basava Tarakam, Bibi Cancer & General Hospital, and Hyderabad Kidney & Laproscopic.

Source: Data extracted from the official website of Arogyasri Trust, 10 December 2011.

Under the scheme, transport charges are to be paid to patients who travel from their home towns to the speciality hospitals located in the urban centres. But our interviews with the patients revealed that they were not paid for to-and-fro transportation charges. The local media has reported that patients have been asked to pay for blood test, medicines and bed charges. For example in Visakhapatnam, Apollo, Care and Seven Hills hospitals collected fee towards bed charges and transport charges. Similarly, it has been reported that several hospitals across the state charge for consultancy, bed and transport facilities from the sick-poor.

Politics of 'Sick-poor' Distribution

As stated earlier, 938 procedures are reimbursed under Arogyasri. While reimbursement for 352 procedures is handled by Star Health and Allied Insurance company, the Arogyasri Health Care Trust manages the reimbursement for the remaining 586. The pre-authorisation and claim settlement for Arogyasri Scheme-I (AS-I) is done by the insurance company, while for Arogyasri Scheme-II (AS-II), it is done by the Arogyasri Trust directly and funded from Chief Minister Relief Fund. Data related to reimbursement of surgeries since the scheme's inception until 8 December 2011 indicates that about 1.4 million surgeries were performed. Of these cases, reimbursements for about 0.7 million surgeries have been provided by the insurance company (AS-I) while reimbursements for the remaining 0.6 million surgeries were handled by the Arogyasri Trust (AS-II). Surprisingly, a large part of AS-I reimbursements were made to private hospitals by the insurance company, while AS-II reimbursements were made to government hospitals by the Arogyasri Trust.

It is evident that certain types of diseases and procedures related to AS-I are being tapped by private hospitals and there seems to be a connection between the reimbursements completed by the insurance company and the procedures conducted by private hospitals. The data indicate that high-cost surgical interventions done by private hospitals in Hyderabad pertain to medical oncology, radiation oncology, surgical oncology, cardiac and CT surgeries, genitor-urinary surgeries, neurosurgery and cochlear implant surgery, which are all listed under AS-I (see Table 4.5). This raises a serious question whether Arogyasri is designed in such a way that most of the high-cost procedures are listed in the domain of insurance company, while the low-cost procedure list has been tasked to the Arogyasri Trust. In a similar study, Rathi *et al.* (2012) indicated that insurance packages do not recognise treatment and care uncertainties that incentivise hospitals to treat simpler and less complicated diseases.

Unnecessary Surgeries

A spurt in unnecessary surgeries has been reported after Arogyasri was launched For instance, in Warangal's 13 private hospitals and 5 government hospitals, 38,090 cases, of which 3,346 operations related to hysterectomy, were reported between 1 August 2008 and 21 August 2010. As there is a scope for quick money to be made in surgeries, private hospitals used rural private practitioners (RMP doctors) to refer poor women with gynaecological problem as hysterectomy cases. Similarly, in the case of neurosurgeries, kidney stones in adults and ulcers, more patients are encouraged to opt for surgical procedures. Earlier, some efforts were made to determine whether these cases could be addressed through non-surgical procedures, but now the easiest option is to direct them for major surgery.

Media reports indicate that there is a widespread culture of commissions, irrational investigations, unnecessary surgical procedures, excessive influence of pharmaceutical companies on prescribing doctors through medical representatives, inflation of hospitalisation bills, holding patients for longer periods to claim higher reimbursement, etc., in various hospitals. These unethical practices had become so rampant that in 2011, the state government stopped payments and launched punitive action against 66 hospitals for committing irregularities while offering treatment to patients under the Arogyasri health insurance scheme.[13]

---

13. Agents include various low-paid employees in both public and private hospitals such as contract workers, security personnel, class IV employees, etc.

Table 4.5

Medical Category-wise Surgeries According to AS-I and AS-II in AP

S.No.	Name of the Surgery/Systems	Total Surgeries as on 08.12.2011 (including Government and Private Hospitals)				Procedural Cost- (Combined List of AS-I and AS-II)
		AS-I	AS-II	Total	%	
1	Medical Oncology	1,62,000	12,142	1,74,142	12.53	800 to 60,000
2	Polytrauma	1,57,993	4093	1,62,086	11.66	3,000 to 1,50,000
3	Cardiac and Cardiothoracic Surgery	1,42,931	6750	1,49,681	10.77	15,000 to 1,50,000
4	General Surgery	0	1,31,753	1,31,753	9.48	10,000 to 80,000
5	Genito Urinary Surgeries	77,570	34,442	1,12,012	8.06	10,000 to 1,40,000
6	Nephrology	0	99,996	99,996	7.19	15,000 to 35,000
7	Neurosurgery	76,085	13,531	89,616	6.44	15,000 to 1,60,000
8	Radiation Oncology	80,833	7175	88,008	6.33	2500 to 1,00,000
9	Gynaecology and Obstetrics Surgery	0	53,964	53,964	3.88	20,000 to 40,000
10	Paediatrics	01	43,749	43,750	3.14	25,000 to 90,000
11	Cardiology	17,931	22,354	40,285	2.89	20,000 to 95,000
12	ENT Surgery	0	39,841	39,841	2.86	10,000 to 50,000
13	Neurology	0	38,687	38,687	2.78	8,000 to 1,00,000
14	Surgical Ontology	29,781	7786	37,567	2.70	3,000 to I,00,000
15	Orthopaedic Surgery and Procedures	10,408	22,349	32,757	2.35	15,000 to 50,000

contd...

...*contd*...

16	Paediatric Surgeries	14,359	7479	21,838	1.57	10,000 to 60,000
17	Plastic Surgery	15,236	2546	17,782	1.27	10,000 to 1,20,000
18	Ophthalmology Surgery	0	15, 701	15,701	1.12	3,000 to 65,000
19	Surgical Gastro-enterology	1007	8411	9418	0.67	25,000 to 1,00,000
20	Gastroenterology	0	8012	8012	0.57	5,000 to 1,50,000
21	Pulmonology	0	7254	7254	0.52	15,000 to 50,000
22	Critical Care	0	6903	6903	0.49	45,000 to 1,20,000
23	General Medicine	03	4281	4284	0.30	20,000 to 50,000
24	Cochlear Implant Surgery	1449	04	1453	0.1	20,000 to 5,20,000
25	Rheumatology	0	1236	1236	0.08	10,000 to 50,000
26	Endocrinology	0	747	747	0.05	12,000 to 1,00,000
27	Dermatology	0	611	611	0.04	20,000 to 30,000
28	Prostheses	72	06	78	0.005	500 to 6,000
29	Infectious Diseases	0	47	47	0.003	20,000 to 25,000
	Total	7,87,659	6,01,850	13,89,509	99.84	

Source: Data extracted from the official website of Arogyasri Trust, 10 December 2011.

Dynamics of Exclusion and Inclusion of Patients

While private hospitals redirect and reject 'unwanted' cases, government hospitals take up all cases under Arogyasri. According to a doctor at Osmania General Hospital,

> Government hospitals have become 'dump yards' of high-risk, low-cost procedures, and hugely complicated cases under Arogyasri. There is tremendous pressure in government hospitals to provide free food,

medicines, longer hospital stay, post-operative follow-up, etc, along with surgery. Denial or lapse of any of these services immediately leads to complaints to higher hospital authorities through local political leaders, Members of Legislative Assembly (MLAs) and Members of Parliament (MPs), not to mention the media.

Similarly, political pressure is exerted on NIMS, an autonomous hospital, to accept all Arogyasri cases including those that exceed the actual cost of procedure as per the defined code. NIMS records indicate that an additional financial burden in such cases is 20-25 per cent above the actual allocation. As the chief minister is the chancellor of NIMS and the fact that several cases are recommended by the chief minister's secretariat (*peshi*), health minister and other political leaders, these patients have to be accepted for treatment. However, there is no scope for political pressure on private and corporate hospitals. An Arogyasri administrator from a government hospital commented: "The sick-poor have a voice in government hospitals, whereas they do not have any voice in private and corporate hospitals; they are simply sent off with no questions entertained." The fact that several non-BPL households have also procured Arogyasri eligibility cards (white card) in rural areas using their clout, their ability to exert pressure on government hospitals is also comparatively high. Selvaraj (2012) argued that publicly funded health insurance schemes beginning from 2007 (including RSBY) and the state-based health insurance schemes appear to have failed to provide financial risk protection to the poor households in the country. Countries such as Brazil and Thailand have invested heavily in strengthening the public health system rather than going in the direction of health insurance which typically promote delivery of services by the private sector.

IV

Discussion

The two main political parties in the state—Telugu Desam and Congress—have pressed ahead with health sector reforms for the last two decades and successfully put 'health' issues on the political agenda. The experiment in restructuring the health care sector through Arogyasri has received wide attention across the country, inciting several state governments to replicate this model. However, a critical scrutiny of this model indicates that the corporate health care industry has effectively staked its claim over the state's allocation of health care resources with very little regulation and accountability. This is done first by redefining the disease categories and legitimising them, and then adding more diseases to the list as appropriate for surgical treatment. In fact, the innovation within the discourse of medical neo-liberalism has been to widen the 'patient-consumer pool' for the corporate health industry. Second, the EMRI made available to the public in case of emergency has been taken over by private health care companies.[14] Third, a major chunk of medical reimbursement of the government employees (Central Government Health Scheme) is harvested by corporate and private hospitals.

Of Andhra Pradesh's health budget of ₹144,710 million between 2008-09 and 2011-12, nearly 25 per cent (₹35,110 million) was allocated to the Arogyasri programme. Instead of additional allocations to Arogyasri, funds were diverted from the existing health budget, depriving the already resource-starved government health network. The expert group on universal health coverage constituted by the Planning Commission of India pointed out that programmes such as Arogyasri, by trying to cater to the high-cost treatment for the BPL population within the limitations of state budget, are grossly neglecting primary and secondary health care (Reddy, 2011).

Arogyasri's focus on specific diseases that require high-cost surgical interventions accounts for less than 2 per cent of the total disease burden. The high incidence of infectious and communicable diseases that cause maximum morbidity and mortality has not been the concern of the new health care model. The skewed logic of high-cost, low frequency, surgical-based interventions has been conceived by design to favour medicines and medical technology over health care providers and seekers. This new culture, politics and economics of health care through Arogyasri redirect funds towards

14. *The Hindu*, 13 December 2011.

surgical procedures in super-specialty hospitals, insurance providers and pharmaceutical companies. This, in turn, facilitates unregulated commercialisation of health care and commodification of the body.

A highly charged social and political environment is created through these health innovations and populist models where diverse participants like health professionals, corporate executives, insurance companies, policy makers, pharmaceutical company representatives, Aarogyamitras, and sick-poor consumers interact. These interactions raise a host of calculable and incalculable hopes, benefits, profits and risks. Arogyasri is a classic example of promoting the interests of the corporate health industry through tertiary hospitals in the public and private sectors in both urban and rural locales, thereby intensifying medicalisation of society in new and complex, techno-scientifically enmeshed ways.

References

Banerji, Debabar (2001). "Landmarks in the Development of Health Services in India", in Imrana Qadeeer, Kasturi Sen and K.R. Nayar (eds.), *Public Health and the Poverty of Reforms.* New Delhi: Sage Publications.

Baru, Rama V. (1998). *Private Health Care in India: Social Characteristics and Trends.* New Delhi: Sage.

———. (2003). "Privatisation of Health Services: A South Asian Perspective", *Economic & Political Weekly* 38(18-24): 4433-37.

Bhore Committee Report (1946). *Government of India Report of the Health Survey and Development Committee.* Vols. I, II, III, IV. New Delhi: Publication Division, Government of India.

Damodaran, Harish (2008). *India's New Capitalists: Caste, Business and Industry in a Modern Nation.* New York: Palgrave Macmillan.

Fisher, A. Jill (2007). "Coming Soon to a Physician Near You: Medical Neoliberalism and Pharmaceutical Clinical Trials", *Harvard Health Policy Review* 8(1): 61-70 (Spring).

Ghosh, Jayati (2006). *Report of the Commission on Farmer's Welfare.* Hyderabad: Government of Andhra Pradesh.

GoAP (1993-94). *A Survey.* Hyderabad: Directorate of Health Services, Government of Andhra Pradesh.

———. (1996). *Fact Sheets.* Hyderabad: Directorate of Health Services, Government of Andhra Pradesh.

———. (1997). *Andhra Pradesh: Four Decades of Development.* Hyderabad: Government of Andhra Pradesh.

———. (2006). *Medium Term Expenditure Framework for Health in AP.* Report submitted to the Department of Health, Medical and Family Welfare, Government of AP, July (cited from Health for the Millions, February-March 2008 and April-May 2008).

HDR (2007). *Human Development Report.* Prepared for Government of Andhra Pradesh. Hyderabad: Centre for Economic and Social Studies.

Mitchell, Andrew, Ajay Mahal and Thomas Bossert (2011). "Health Care Utilisation in Rural Andhra Pradesh", *Economic & Political Weekly* XLVI (5): 15-19, 20 January.

Narayana, K.V. (2003). "Size and Nature of Health-care System", in C.H. Hanumantha Rao and S. Mahendra Dev (eds.), *Andhra Pradesh Development: Economic Reforms and Challenges Ahead.* Hyderabad: Centre for Economics and Social Studies (CESS).

———. (2009). "Public and Private Mix in Medical Care: Changing Patterns in Andhra Pradesh", in S. Mahendra Dev, C. Ravi and M. Venkatanarayana (eds.), *Human Development in AP Experiences: Issues and Challenges.* Hyderabad: CESS.

Prasad, N. Purendra (2007). "Medicine, Power and Social Legitimacy: A Socio-Historical Appraisal of Health Systems in Contemporary India", *Economic & Political Weekly* XLII (34): 3491-98.

———. (2014). "Changing Structure of Governance in Non-Metropolitan Cities: A Study in Andhra Pradesh", *Economic and Political Weekly* XLIX(22): 83-91, May 31.

Raja Reddy, D. (2008). "A Critical Evaluation of the Health Policies of the Present Government and Suggestions for Their Improvement", in *Health Sector Reforms and their Impact on People.* Jana Vignana Vedika, Hyderabad, Doctors for People's Health and AP Medical and Sales Representatives Union.

Rathi, Pratheek, Arnab Mukherji and Gita Sen (2012). "Rashtriya Swasthya Bima Yojana: Evaluation, Utilisation, Roll-out and Perceptions in Amaravati District, Maharashtra", *Economic and Political Weekly* XLVII(39): 57-64.

Sarma, E.A.S (2004). "Is Rural Economy Breaking Down: Farmers Suicides in Andhra Pradesh", *Economic & Political Weekly* XXXIX(28): 3087-89.

Selvaraj, Sakthivel (2012). "Publicly Financed Health Insurance Schemes: Ignorance is not Bliss", *Economic & Political Weekly* XLVII(29): 109-11, July 21.

Shukla, Rajan, Veena Shatrugna and R. Srivatsan (2011). "Arogyasri Health Care Model: Advantage Private Sector", *Economic & Political Weekly* XLVI (49): 38-42, December 3.

Special Correspondent (2014). "Poor Health Care ups Private Spending", *The Hindu*, 18 July.

Reddy, Srinath (2011). "High Level Expert Group Report on Universal Health Coverage for India", *Planning Commission of India*, New Delhi.

Upadhya, Carol (1997) "Social and Cultural Strategies of Class Formation in Coastal Andhra Pradesh", *Contributions to Indian Sociology* (NS) 31(2): 169-93.

Vijay, G. (2012). "The Business of Health Care and the Challenge of Health Security: The Case of Arogyasri Health Insurance Programme in Andhra Pradesh" in K.P. Kannan and Jan Breman (ed.), *The Long Road to Social Security*. New Delhi: OUP.

Zachariah, Anand, R. Srivatsan and Susie Tharu (2010). *Towards a Critical Medical Practice – Reflections on the Dilemmas of Medical Culture Today.* Hyderabad: Orient Blackswan.

5

ANKITA MUKHERJEE

The Rashtriya Swasthya Bima Yojana

An Overview

Health financing is one of the critical determinants of access to health care in a country. Insurance is one of the many ways of health financing available. There can be varying role of the state in financing and provisioning of health care in the different types of health systems. While the United Kingdom (UK) has largely public provision and financing through the National Health Services, Germany has a mandatory social insurance for its working population where the state has important role in regulating and pooling of funds. In the United States (US), health care costs are met through purchase of private insurance with the state playing a minimal role. In India, a highly fragmented health financing system exists, with health care being largely privately financed through OOP (out-of-pocket) expenditure. About 80 per cent of health expenses are met through OOP payments in India (Baru *et al.*, 2010). It has been estimated that 32.5 million people (25.5 million in rural and 7 million in urban areas) are pushed below the poverty line as a result of making OOP payments (Garg and Karan, 2009).

In the recent past, medical insurance as an alternative means of financing health care and a viable means of providing financial risk protection has gained importance. This is evident from increase in the government financed medical insurance schemes in many states like Kerala,[1] Tamil Nadu,[2] Karnataka[3] and Andhra Pradesh (AP)[4] and

1. Rashtriya Swasthaya Bima Yojana (RSBY)/Comprehensive Health Insurance Scheme (CHIS).
2. Chief Minister's Comprehensive Health Insurance Scheme, previously the Chief Minister Kalaignar Insurance Scheme for life-saving treatments.
3. Yeshasvini Co-operative Farmers Health Care Scheme.
4. Rajeev Arogyasri Scheme.

introduction of the nationwide RSBY scheme for the BPL (below poverty line) families. Most of these schemes are limited to tertiary level or secondary level hospitalisation.

Although RSBY is not the first scheme that is aimed at providing large-scale public insurance, previous efforts have not been as successful as RSBY.[5] Compared to its predecessor—the Universal Health Insurance Scheme (UHIS)—the RSBY has achieved impressive enrolment ratios in a short span of four years. This chapter will examine key features of its design and implementation which have contributed to its successful coverage. It will also review recent studies on utilisation trends that have been undertaken across the countries and highlight some key issues that emerged during a study in Uttar Pradesh (UP).

Key Features of the Rashtriya Swasthya Bima Yojna

The RSBY is a national level insurance scheme for the BPL families, in which the government subsidises the premium. It is an insurance scheme that primarily focuses on the BPL population in India that has been categorised by the Planning Commission. The scheme, therefore, can potentially reach a population of about 300 million. The scheme has been able to reach around 22.7 million families (approximately 80 million beneficiaries) in a short span of four years, since its launch in April 2008, which is quite remarkable (Public Health Foundation of India [PFHI], 2011). In a recent newspaper report, the coverage is claimed to be 28 million families (*Economic Times*, April 2012). This in itself is a very large number, especially if we consider the limited coverage that other state-funded insurance schemes like Employees State Insurance Scheme (ESIS) have been able to achieve in the several decades of their existence.[6]

5. The Universal Health Insurance Scheme was announced in 2003. It provided health coverage up to ₹30,000, life insurance in case of death due to accident up to ₹25,000 and ₹50 per day (up to 11 days) as loss of livelihood in case of an illness. It was meant for both BPL (below poverty line) and APL (above poverty line) families and individuals, and the government subsidised only part of the premium for BPL. The scheme had very low take up (0.4 million families) and very low utilisation rates (Ahuja and Narang, 2005).

6. As per 2009-10 data, there are 14.3 million families (55.4 million beneficiaries) covered by the ESIS (PHFI, 2011).

[The government has also announced its intention to extend its coverage to informal sector workers like domestic workers, *beedi* workers and National Rural Employment Guarantee Act (NREGA) workers.] However, from the point of view of a health financing mechanism that provides universal coverage to all citizens, this scheme is nowhere close.

As per documents on its website, the main objectives of RSBY are to provide financial security to BPL households from hospitalisation-related expenses, improve access to quality health care, provide beneficiaries the power of choice to select a health care provider and provide a scheme which is transparent and simple to use for the end user. There are some important features in the design of the scheme which are discussed below.

Use of Biometric Technology and Digitalisation of Claim Settlement

RSBY provides coverage for up to five members of a BPL household including the head of the household, the spouse and three dependents. Each family is provided with a biometric card that stores fingerprints of all the five members who get enrolled. In case of any illness, the family can go to any empanelled hospital and seek treatment. The hospital must verify the identity of the beneficiary by taking his/her fingerprint and matching it with that stored in the card. After verifying identity of the patient, he/she is provided treatment free of cost. This way the scheme aims to provide its beneficiaries cashless treatment. The scheme is of course limited only to those conditions which require hospitalisation. A list of 780 procedures has been prepared which are covered under RSBY. Some surgical procedures that do not require hospitalisation (like cataract) are also included in the list. For each of these procedures, a predicted package rate has been fixed. Once the treatment is over, the hospital submits its claims to the insurance company or the TPA (third party administrator), which in turn reimburses the hospital as per the package rates. Claims are submitted and settled digitally, ensuring minimal paperwork.

Coverage of Pre-existing Illnesses and Some Non-medical Costs

One of the most significant features of the scheme is that pre-existing illnesses are covered. Private insurance companies often exclude this to maximise their profit. To facilitate cashless treatment, RSBY package rates (that are reimbursed to the hospitals) include not only doctor's fee, bed charges and food, but also expenses incurred for diagnostic tests and medicines up to one day before admission of the patient as well as up to five days from the day of discharge from the hospital. It provides travel allowance of ₹100 per hospitalisation, up to a maximum of ₹1,000 to the family of the patient. The insurance company is paid the premium by the government for every family enrolled. The scheme is funded by the central and state governments, with the former bearing 75 per cent and the state government bearing 25 per cent of the cost. In Jammu & Kashmir (J&K) and the northeastern states, the centre bears 90 per cent while the state government bears 10 per cent of the cost.

Public-Private Partnership (PPP) Model

The scheme is run in a PPP model with the central government, state government and insurance agencies as actors in functioning of the scheme. What makes RSBY different from other schemes is the formulation of this scheme as a business model, with incentives for key players and the extensive use of technology to administer this scheme (Jain, 2010). Insurance agencies implementing the scheme can be private or public. A large number of private hospitals has been empanelled to provide medical care to RSBY beneficiaries.

These design features are important because they eventually shape the user experience and will determine long-term sustainability of the scheme.

Process Flow and Important Stakeholders

RSBY involves multiple players at different levels to implement the programme. While the central government is involved in planning and funding the scheme, actual implementation at the village level is undertaken by private players (insurance companies/TPAs). The state government and the nodal agency, that it sets up, help in oversight and devising state specific guidelines. Their actual role in implementation is limited though not entirely absent. They invite bids, manage contract and appoint FKOs (field key officers) who are present during enrolment. However the larger role at the ground level implementation is left to the private parties. Key stakeholders and their role has been explained diagrammatically in Figure 5.1.

Figure 5.1

Key Stakeholders and Process Flow of RSBY

Ministry of Labour and Employment (GoI)	• *Planning:* Designing different aspects of the scheme, setting guidelines and parametres (e.g., reimbursement rates, empanelment criteria, etc.). • *Financing:* Providing funds to state government, financial management and planning • *Monitoring:* Monitoring state and national level utilisation and related information
State Government	• *Planning:* Make modifications to parametres set by the central government if required • *Financing:* Partly finance the scheme (most states contribute 25% of funds) • *Implementation:* Set up a State Nodal Agency which is responsible for ensuring proper implementation and monitoring in the state
State Nodal Agency	• *Implementation:* Select Insurance Agengcies (IAs) through competitive bidding process and provide terms of contract including fixing premium rates, provide updated BPL list to IAs, appoint FKOs who are present during enrolment, set up District Kiosk and undertake information campaigns. • *Monitoring:* Monitor enrolment process, financial monitoring, monitor contract terms with IAs and monitor state level enrolment data.
Insurance Agency	• *Implementation:* Select smart card providers, carry out enrolment process in the villages, provide staff for the District Kiosk, operate a helpline for users, empanel hospitals, settle claims and reimburse hospitals. IAs can appoint a TPA which takes up the responsibility of processing claims. • *Monitoring:* Ensure veracity of claims filed and that hospitals fulfil criteria for empanelment.
Provider (Hospital)	• Provision of medical services to RSBY beneficiaries

Source: Based on information provided in RSBY website (*www.rsby.gov.in*).

At the centre, the primary responsibility of planning and monitoring is with the Ministry of Labour and Employment

(MoLE), Government of India (GoI). The MoLE has designed the key features of the scheme with technical assistance from the German development agency, GTZ (Deutsche Gesellschaft für Technische Zusammenarbeit) and the World Bank. However the MoLE is not directly responsible for its implementation. Implementation is at the state level for states which want to adopt the scheme. Every state has to set up an independent state nodal agency (SNA) which has the primary responsibility of oversight and maintenance of enrolment data. The SNA is also responsible for sending detailed information about the implementation of the programme to the MoLE. The SNA invites tenders by insurance companies. Both public as well as private insurance companies can bid. Separate tenders can be invited for separate districts from a cluster of districts or the state as a whole. Cost premium is decided for different districts separately. On acceptance of the tender, the insurance company enters into a contract with the SNA.

It is then the insurance company's responsibility to find a smart card provider (SCP) who fulfils the specifications laid down in the programme. Insurance agencies may also appoint a TPA, whose job is to monitor the network hospitals and ensure validity of the claims before reimbursement is made. The TPA and the SCP therefore enter into a contract with the insurance company.

Empanelment of hospitals is the responsibility of the insurance company. The RSBY lays down certain minimum criteria for empanelment of hospitals.

The criteria for empanelling private hospitals and health facilities are (Sethi, 2011):

- At least 10 inpatient medical beds for primary inpatient health care.
- Fully equipped and engaged in providing medical and surgical facilities, including diagnostic facilities, i.e., pathology testing and X-ray, electrocardiogram (ECG), etc., for the care and treatment of injured or sick persons as inpatients.
- A fully equipped operating theatre where surgical operations are carried out.

- Fully qualified, round the clock, doctors and nurses.
- Basic record keeping to furnish details of the insured patient to the insurer or its representative/government/trust, as and when required.
- Registration with income tax department.
- Telephone/fax and internet facilities and smart card readers.

The insurance agency enters into a contract with the private hospitals that are empanelled. For empanelment of the public hospitals, the insurance company has to get approval from the state health department to participate and then contact government hospitals.

The private hospitals that are willing to be part of the RSBY network have to bear the cost of setting up required equipment, hardware and software to read the biometric card of the beneficiary and undertake paperless transaction. It is however the responsibility of the insurance company to set up the required equipment for the government hospitals.

Enrolment is done at the village level itself by the SCP or the insurance company. Currently, the BPL list as per the BPL survey of 2002 is being used. It is the responsibility of the SNA to provide the BPL list to the insurance agency. The insurance company uses this list to make enrolments. The insurance company should make arrangements to announce beforehand the day and place of enrolment and put up a list of eligible families at a public place. On the day of enrolment, the beneficiary family has to come to the enrolment booth along with family members being enrolled. Their fingerprints are taken and the card should be handed over then and there along with a booklet/pamphlet providing information about empanelled hospitals, conditions and other details of the scheme. During enrolment, a government appointed official called the FKO who is appointed by the SNA, must be present. It is the FKO's responsibility to oversee that the enrolment being carried out by the insurance company is in compliance with the scheme's provisions. The FKO must also ensure that the correct person (as per the BPL list) is being enrolled, by asking for identity proof or asking the *pradhan* to be present to verify identity of the person. After the smart card is issued, the FKO must validate the card by inserting his/her smart card and providing his/her fingerprint.

Every district must also have a district kiosk set up by the SNA and staffed and managed by the insurance company. The district kiosk should have all district level data. It is also the place where duplicate cards (splitting of cards) can be generated for families of migrant labourers. The insurance company also has to set up a 24-hour helpline to assist those who want to use the card.

The hospitals can conduct health camps to attract RSBY card holders to utilise the scheme. NGOs (non-governmental organisation) can also be involved by the insurance agency for generating awareness about the scheme. RSBY therefore has multiple players who perform different functions for the implementation of the scheme. What is important to take note here is that the entire scheme has been designed as a business model with incentives built in for private players. The participation of private players and success of the PPP model therefore will be dependent on the continuation of steady profits.

Trends in Utilisation of RSBY

RSBY was started in 2008 in some select districts. As of May 2011, it was operational in 229 districts in 22 states of India. In May 2011, 182 districts had completed one year of implementation of RSBY, while 47 districts had completed two years of implementation. Currently, the scheme has been implemented in 440 districts across 26 states and two union territories as per the RSBY official website. At the last count, there were more than 32 million individuals enrolled under the scheme with more than 41 thousand cases of hospitalisation.[7] There have been several studies to evaluate different aspects of the scheme, including several working papers and evaluation studies commissioned by the MoLE itself. Most of these studies enquire into enrolment levels, profile of enrolling families, awareness levels, hospitalisation pattern and user satisfaction (MacDonald, 2011a; 2011b; Amicus Advisory Pvt Ltd, 2010; 2011).

7. Based on information provided in *www.rsby.gov.in* as on 17 October 2012.

There have been relatively fewer studies that have tried to assess the impact on reducing OOP expenditure (Amicus Advisory Pvt Ltd, 2010; Shahrawat and Rao, 2011; Selvaraj and Karan, 2012).

Studies which have enquired into the question of OPP expenditure found that despite having enrolled in RSBY, users have had OOP expenditure. One study done in Durg district of Chhattisgarh shows that more than one-third of the beneficiaries who utilised the RSBY incurred OOP expenses. On an average, users spent ₹686 with an average OOP expenditure of ₹309 in public hospitals and ₹1,079 in private hospitals (Nandi *et al.*, 2012). There were similar findings in Delhi as well where more than one-third of users interviewed had spent money out of their pocket. On an average, RSBY beneficiaries in Delhi spent ₹1,690. Another study has tried to assess the impact of RSBY on reducing OOP expenditure by comparing average medical expenses of RSBY beneficiaries and non-beneficiaries in Jaunpur district of UP. It was found that RSBY users on an average spent much less on their illness (₹556) than non-users (₹2,759) (Amicus Advisory Pvt Ltd., 2010). There is however need for more studies on the impact of RSBY on reducing OOP expenditure and providing financial risk protection.

Enrolment rates in different studies were seen to vary. A recent evaluation study found that the average conversion ratio[8] in 229 districts (in 22 states) in May 2011 was 51.2 per cent (Krishnaswamy and Ruchismita, 2011). This means that the scheme has been able to reach about half of the BPL families it targeted. There has been a minor improvement in enrolment over the previous year. An earlier study had found that enrolment ratios in 24 districts in January 2010 were 49.6 per cent (Sun, 2010). There are however wide variations in enrolment ratios among states, among districts and indeed at the village level. The conversion ratio in some states like Tripura is as high as 87 per cent, whereas in Assam it is only 11 per cent. In UP, conversion ratio was 53 per cent. (Krishnaswamy and Ruchismita, 2011). On comparing district level data, it was found that some districts like Bharuch in Gujarat (66.3%) and Fatehabad (69.7%)

8. Ratio of number of households enrolled to total number of eligible BPL families per district.

and Jind (68.1%) in Haryana, reported relatively high enrolment ratios. Other districts like Gonda (35.3%) in UP, Jalgaon (32.7%) in Maharashtra and Faridabad (32.2%) in Haryana reported very low enrolment ratios (Sun, 2010).

One problem during enrolment that has been commonly reported is exclusion of poor and inclusion of non-poor due to the deficiencies in the BPL list. A study in Jaunpur district found that about 40 per cent of the respondents reported absence of their names in the BPL list and 31 per cent of non-enrollees had BPL cards (Amicus Advisory Pvt Ltd, 2010). It is also well known that the BPL list often includes non-poor who are powerful enough to use unfair means or connections to get their names in the BPL list. One study in Karnataka reported that during enrolment, in every village there were some people who were provoked by inclusion of persons who were generally not perceived as poor. Angry residents approached enrolment officers to question the provision of benefits meant for the poor to the relatively wealthy and the police had to be called in at many places (Rajashekhar *et al.*, 2011). Another problem with the BPL list is that the current BPL list has data from the BPL survey done almost 10 years ago. Using an old list also means exclusion of those who were born after 2002-03. Those who migrated would still be part of the list and women who have got married into a household after 2002-03 would not have been part of the list.

There is wide variation in utilisation rates. But it has been found that hospitalisation rates under RSBY are more than the average hospitalisation rates in the country. Overall hospitalisation ratio of RSBY was found to be 2.4 per cent (of all enrolled individuals in all 229 districts). It was higher than what National Sample Survey (NSS) 2004 reported as the hospitalisation rates of low income segments at the national level, 1.7 per cent. There were however large variations among states in hospitalisation rates. It ranged from 0.1 per cent in Assam to 5.2 per cent in Kerala (in the first year of operation) (Krishnaswamy and Ruchismita, 2011).

Almost all the evaluation studies as well as independent studies found that awareness about the scheme was limited. This was seen in awareness related to different aspects of the scheme like the amount for which cover was provided, hospitals empanelled, provision of travel allowance and provision for free medicines. [MacDonald, 2011a; 2011b; Amicus Advisory Pvt Ltd, 2010; 2011; Krishnaswamy and Ruchismita, 2011; CTRD, 2012; Nandi *et al.*, 2012].

Evaluation studies also found that some of the provisions in the scheme like providing smart card on the day of enrolment, providing pamphlet or booklet with list of benefits, claims processing procedure and network hospitals were not followed (MacDonald, 2011a; 2011b; Amicus Advisory Pvt Ltd, 2010; 2011; Krishnaswamy and Ruchismita, 2011; CTRD, 2012; Rajashekhar *et al.*, 2011).

A review of utilisation pattern shows that although RSBY has reached an enormous population, it is only a fraction of the BPL population that it targets to cover. There is wide variation in enrolment ratios and utilisation rates. Certain problems have also come to light, for instance extremely low levels of awareness of different aspects of the scheme will impact utilisation. There have been shortcomings in implementation. In many places, smart cards are not being provided on the day of enrolment neither is printed information being provided about empanelled institutions. These problems highlight poor oversight during enrolment, despite building in a monitoring mechanism in the programme design.

Some Emerging Issues: Reflections from a Micro Study

There have already been several large-scale surveys undertaken to evaluate different aspects of the scheme. A qualitative study was done in Sitapur district of UP to assess the experience of utilisation of the scheme by its beneficiaries. Twenty-three persons who had utilised the smart card were interviewed, out of which 20 had visited a private hospital and 3 had visited a government hospital. Doctors from the respective hospitals were also interviewed. The findings corroborated the gaps in implementation that had emerged from the various evaluation studies done earlier. However the study also threw up some areas of concern related to the design of the programme. Some of the areas that need reflection have been discussed here.

The Hidden Costs of 'Cashless Hospitalisation'

One of the most novel features of the RSBY scheme is the provision of 'cashless hospitalisation' to its beneficiaries. In an event of hospitalisation, presenting his/her card to an empanelled hospital should ensure free admission and surgery. Since the insurance cover also includes diagnostic tests, free medicines up to five days from the day of discharge, provision for free food as well as a travel allowance, it is expected to provide cashless hospitalisation. Already studies have highlighted that even RSBY beneficiaries have to spend certain amounts of money from out of their own pocket. The study in Sitapur shows that to truly understand the scheme's potential for providing financial risk protection, there is need to look beyond the single episode of hospitalisation for which RSBY was utilised. For many of the patients, already large amounts had been spent before utilising RSBY because poor families often consult a range of providers before ending up in the RSBY empanelled institution. This is despite the fact that they had the card with them for a year. It is clear therefore that in the absence of information, having the smart card could not by itself ensure reduction in OOP expenditure. (There were of course many cases where the condition has existed for several years before the scheme started and the family has already spent large sums of money.) Even during hospitalisation, indirect costs often add up to much more than what is covered by the travel allowance. Expenses on travel and food for caretakers of the patient are an additional burden. Sometimes particular diagnostic tests are not available in the facility, as was the case in a community health centre (CHC) and are prescribed outside. When poor and illiterate patients go to diagnostic centres in small towns, they are not given any bills and they themselves have little power to negotiate for bills. In the absence of bills, they are not able to be reimbursed by the hospital and have to bear these costs themselves. While most of the expenses during hospitalisation are covered, post-hospitalisation costs are not entirely covered. The study in Sitapur showed that a health condition leads to expenses even before and after the event of hospitalisation. Since RSBY is a scheme that primarily offers surgical services, it is quite natural that the patient may need to visit the hospital several times after the surgery to get their stitches cut or get dressing for their wounds. Medication may continue much beyond the five days for which there is provision for free medicine. There have also been cases where free medicines have not been provided after discharge or have been provided for only two days. A recent study in Chhattisgarh found that around 48.2 per cent of the smart card holders reported continuing their treatment after discharge from hospitals (CTRD, 2012). Clearly, there are expenses involved despite having a smart card. To what extent the scheme is able to provide financial risk protection therefore needs a framework that does not restrict itself to a single event of hospitalisation. What is crucial to understand is that hospitalisation is an event that has both a history and a future.

Focus on Secondary Care Procedures: A Fragmented Approach

RSBY is clearly a scheme that focuses on secondary care procedures and not outpatient care or tertiary care. Given the extremely low levels of awareness about the finer details of the scheme, a smart card holder is often led to believe that the card can be used for any illness. When he takes the card to the hospital for a condition that does not require hospitalisation (one that can be dealt with outpatient care), either he is refused treatment or must pay out of pocket. The other option—which has been exercised in several cases by doctors—is admitting the patient under 'general ward' category. The general ward category under the RSBY package provides for two days of hospitalisation for some chronic conditions as well as infectious diseases that mostly require outpatient treatment but sometimes need hospitalisation. Some of the diseases included in this category are asthma, bronchitis, typhoid, malaria, pneumonia, diabetes, diarrhoea and hypertension. It is likely that conditions which could have been treated through outpatient care are also included in this category thereby leading to over medicalisation and increasing costs. The other side of the story as narrated by doctors (and through personal observation) is that when patients come with the smart card, they expect some kind of free treatment. Some patients hope to get free diagnostic tests and medicines therefore don't mind undergoing admission. Sometimes doctors take the decision to admit the patient because the beneficiary requests them on grounds of poverty. Raw data show that a significant number of patients who were treated under RSBY were admitted as general ward patients which is meant for non-surgical treatment. Data of beneficiaries between July and October 2011[9] show that there were 553 beneficiaries who utilised the RSBY scheme. Out of these, 185 cases were treated under general ward while 368 were surgical cases. In other words, about 33 per cent or one-third of patients used RSBY for non-surgical cases even though the scheme is primarily meant for surgical cases. If we further analyse the conditions that were admitted under the 'general ward,' we see an interesting pattern. Out of the 185 cases, two conditions namely abdomen pain and fever make up about 60 per cent of the cases. While abdomen pain is an ambiguous category, one wonders if all the fever cases required hospitalisation. The fact that this category is also being used for post-operative cases is also a revelation. The RSBY package specifies the number of days for which a patient can be admitted for each condition. It is possible that in certain cases, the number of days that is specified is not enough for the patient to recover. In such conditions, perhaps this category provides the flexibility to extend hospitalisation for patients who need it.

The study also found a number of patients with chronic conditions like tuberculosis (TB) or chronic obstructive pulmonary disease (COPD) who visited hospitals to get treatment. In such cases, though they could be temporary relieved from symptoms like breathlessness, there was disappointment at not getting treatment for their condition over a long period. Treatment seeking by patients with conditions like TB raises important questions. There is already a national programme for TB in place. However, the private hospitals in which the patients seek treatment are in no way accountable to the national health programmes. It was seen that patients would get treated under general ward and then discontinue treatment because it was too expensive, whereas they should follow a standardised

9. The sample for the study was selected out of beneficiaries who had used the RSBY card in this period. See also, Table 5.1.

regimen of drugs. There seems to be a situation where RSBY is focusing on one goal of the health system namely providing financial risk protection, while it is not in sync with the other goal namely ensuring public health. There needs to be greater reflection on seeing where RSBY fits in the health system and how it can further its goals.

Figure 5.2

Condition for which Patients were Admitted under 'General Ward': Based on Total Cases of Hospitalisation between July and October 2012 in Sitapur District

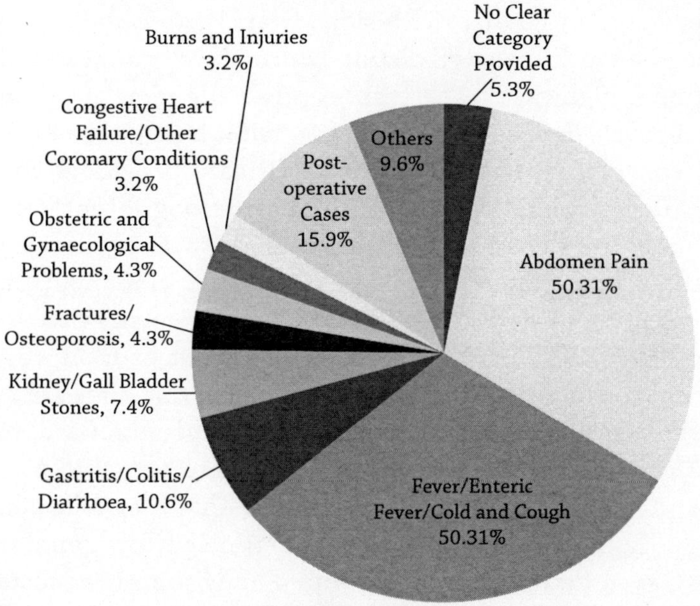

Source: Based on utilisation data obtained from MoLE/GIZ.

The perception of beneficiaries regarding the scheme was also dependent on the condition for which they sought treatment. Those who had a pre-existing condition that required surgery or emergency care were extremely satisfied. Those with chronic conditions were not satisfied as the scheme did not cater to their needs.

Courting the Private Sector: The Problems

One of the important objectives of RSBY is to provide its users with choice so that they are able to choose good quality care. This has been achieved through the mechanism of PPP, whereby a number of private hospitals have been included in the network of hospitals. The design of RSBY is a business model with an built-in mechanism for incentives and checks which is expected to make the programme sustainable. But the market logic of choice is quite redundant in remote areas and poorer districts as was seen in the case of Sitapur district. In this district, all except one private provider is concentrated in the district headquarter. There is only one private hospital in a block town—Sidhauli, which is well connected through the national highway to the state capital. The more geographically remote districts depend entirely on the public health system. Another area of concern is the perception of private providers about the scheme. The entire model of PPP rests on strong incentives for the private providers to be a part of this scheme. However there is a sense of dissatisfaction related to package rates, delay in reimbursement of claims, rejection of claims and additional requirements that are being set. Since the RSBY package rate includes cost of food, tests, bed charge and consultation, private providers feel that they are not able to recover cost. (The current package rate for 'general ward' category is ₹500 per day.) Since private providers are not able to recover costs in one day of admission, it is possible that they take admission for three days (the maximum that is allowed for 'general ward' patients), even though it is unwarranted, only to recover costs. In an unregulated health care market, private hospitals often invest money on diagnostic equipment, etc., and recover costs by setting arbitrary rates. In the case of many private providers therefore, RSBY is not able to provide them enough monetary incentive by setting package rates at levels much lower than what they are used to charging. The other reason for dissatisfaction, namely hurdles in reimbursement of claims, has to be understood within the context of the business model to which the scheme adheres. The insurance company which reimburses the hospitals has an incentive in curbing excessive claims so that it does not face losses. Insurance agencies have transferred

Table 5.1

Costs Incurred Prior to During and After Hospitalisation under RSBY

Respondent Name (Names have been Changed)	*Condition/Symptoms Reported by User for which Treatment was Sought*	*Illness Diagnosed/ Treatment Provided (as Specified by Provider)*	*Number of Providers Visited Before RSBY (Including Qualified and Unqualified)*	*Approximate Amount Spent in Rupees on Treatment Prior to using RSBY*	*Approximate Amount Spent in Rupees During RSBY Treatment (Break up where Available)**	*Approximate Amount Spent in Rupees After Hospitalisation (till Jan 2012)*	*Amount Booked in Rupees under RSBY Package*
Mangal (Late)	Tuberculosis	Enteric fever	4	40,000###	NA	Nil	1500
Ramrati	High fever, body ache	Enteric fever	1	600#	2000 (1st time) (medicies, food, travel), 1000 (2nd time) (travel and food)	Nil	1000
Narendra	Swelling in legs and hands	Chronic Hepatitis	5	7000-7500#	1000 (tests and travel), Travel only=200	Nil	1000
Chhote Lal	Difficulty in breathing	Fever	1	80-100#	Nil	300	1000
Sunita	Increased heart palpitation, shivering of her hands and fainting	Pain in abdomen	4	90,000###	200 (travel and food)		1000

contd...

...contd...

Puja	Fever, numbness in leg and hand	Post-operation	Nil	Nil	Nil	1700	1000
Ram Ratan	Tuberculosis	Cough and pain in body	2	2000-3000##	NA	15,000	1000
Preeti	Unknown	Enteric fever	8**##	55,000-60,000**##	400 (travel)	>1000	1000
Reeta	Pain abdomen	Pain in abdomen	3	6000##	100 (food)	>500	1500
Jagjeevan Prasad	Severe and disabling pain in the stomach, breathlessness and difficulty in movement and active work	Enteric fever	**	>40,000**##	NA	360	1000
Suraj	Swelling	Abdominal peri-tal wall abscess/ abscess drainage	2	1500#	Nil	300	2000
Ram Charan	Pain in the stomach	Right side hernia/ hernioplasty	Nil	Nil	2500-3000 (food, travel, medicines), Food and travel only=50	NA	7000

contd...

...contd...

Rani	Gluteal abscess	Right Side gluteal abscess/ Drainage of Abscess	Nil	Nil	500-600 (travel)	450	2000
Lallan (Late)	High fever (was diagnosed as TB positive)	Fever	Nil	Nil	200 (travel and food)	Nil	1000
Ramkali	Muscular pain in hands and legs and fever	Fever	6	3000-3500###	300 (food)	Nil	1000
Pyarelal	Poor function of kidneys and difficulty in breathing (COPD)	Bonchitis	several**	**	230 (food)	Upto 30,000	1000
Ramesh	Piles and anal fissure	Piles and anal fissure/fissurectomy and haemorrhoidectomy	1	2500**#	2500 (travel and food)	Nil	11250
Nankai	Pain in the Stomach	Bulky uterus (later hysterectomy done)	2	7000-8000###	400 (travel)	> 300	1000
Champa Kumari	Cough, breathlessness and fever (was diagnosed as TB positive)	Pain in chest	3	9250##	600 (travel)	500 -600	1000

contd...

...contd...

Ram Pyari	Hypertension (sleeplessness, restlessness, dizzyness)	Enteric fever	2	200##	200 (food)	3300	1000
Samir	Hydrocoel	Hydrocoel/ Hydrocelectomy excision	2	300-350#	Nil	600-700	4000
Kamlawati	High fever, gas formation and pain in the body	Fever	Nil	Nil	30 (travel and food)	Nil	1500
Sultana	Water broke in late pregnancy	Normal delivery	1	350#	50 (medicines/ registration)	Nil	2500

Note: No specified time frame was given for calculating OOP expenditure.
NA: respondent not able to recall/data missing.
*Amount after deducting ₹100 received as travel allowance.
** Does not recall as problem exists for past ten years.
**#Money spent over past five years.
Money spent over past one year.
**## Money spent over past ten years.
#Money spent over past two years.
Money spent over past three years.

the job of reimbursements to agencies known as TPAs. The TPAs are paid by the insurance company and are expected to keep losses for the insurance agency at bay. This has translated into rejection of claims by the TPA, clearly aimed at reducing costs for the insurance company that hires it. Providers complain that many rejections are unfair and made on flimsy grounds. Another alarming trend that was reported by a private provider was that the TPA had made reimbursement conditional on the production of certain documents. These include a photocopy of the RSBY card holder's BPL card and his/her photo. This defeats the spirit of the scheme as a paperless and cashless scheme. Poor patients bear the repercussion by having to travel back several kilometres to get their ration cards and spend money out of their pocket on photographs. The requirement for BPL card is also confusing because the beneficiaries of the RSBY are those who have been selected as BPL in the Planning Commission's list, whereas BPL cards are given to beneficiaries who are categorised as such in the state's BPL survey. While there are certainly overlaps, it is not necessary that all RSBY enrollees are BPL card holders. It seems that it is the poorest that end up suffering in this complex design of incentives and disincentive.

The RSBY is a unique scheme which has made a remarkable achievement in reaching out to an enormous population in a relatively short span. There are however concerns related to both its implementation and design. It has been successful in reducing cost of undergoing certain surgical procedures for a large number of beneficiaries, but there is still a long way to go in providing complete financial risk protection. There is need for constant research and reflection on different aspects of the scheme to make it more relevant.

References

Ahuja, R. and Alka Narang (2005). "Emerging Trend in Health Insurance for Low Income Groups", *Economic and Political Weekly* XL(38).

Amicus Advisory Private Limited (2010). *Rashtriya Swasthya Bima Yojana: Studying Jaunpur (Uttar Pradesh)*. Evaluation study commissioned by MoLE, GoI. Accessed from *http://www.rsby.gov.in/Documents.aspx?ID=14* (accessed on 15 May 2012).

———. (2011). *Evaluation Study of Rashtriya Swasthya Bima Yojana in Shimla & Kangra Districts in Himachal Pradesh*. Evaluation study commissioned by MoLE, GoI. Accessed from *http://www.rsby.gov.in/Documents.aspx?ID=14* (accessed on 15 May 2012).

Baru, R., A.K. Shiva Kumar, Arnab Acharya, K. Nagaraj and Sanghmitra Acharya (2010). "Inequities in Access to Health Services in India: Caste, Class and Religion", *Economic and Political Weekly* XLV(38): 49-58.

CTRD (2012). *Final Report on Evaluation of "Rashtriya Swasthya Bima Yojana" in Chhattisgarh*. Submitted to State Nodal Agency, RSBY Chhattisgarh, Department of Health and Family Welfare, Raipur

Garg, C. and A.K. Karan (2009). "Reducing Out-of-pocket Expenditures to Reduce Poverty: A Disaggregated Analysis at Rural-urban and State Level in India", *Health Policy and Planning* 24: 116-28

Jain, N. (2010). *56 Million Steps towards Universal Coverage: RSBY Health Insurance for the Poor in India*. Frankfurt, Germany: GTZ.

Krishnaswamy, K. and R. Ruchismita (2011). "Performance Trends and Policy Recommendations: An Evaluation of the Mass Health Insurance Scheme of Government of India", *RSBY Working Paper*. Accessed from *http://www.rsby.gov.in/Documents.aspx?ID=14* (accessed on 15 May 2012).

MacDonald, Mott (2011a). *Pilot Post-enrolment Survey of the RSBY Program in Gujarat*. Evaluation study commissioned by MoLE, GoI. Accessed from *http://www.rsby.gov.in/Documents.aspx?ID=14* (accessed on 15 May 2012).

———. (2011b). *Pilot Post-enrolment Survey of the RSBY Program in Haryana*. Evaluation study commissioned by MoLE, GoI. Accessed from *http://www.rsby.gov.in/Documents.aspx?ID=14* (accessed on 15 May 2012).

Nandi, S., M. Nundy, V. Prasad, K. Kanungo, H. Khan, S. Haripriya, T. Mishra and S. Garg (2012). "The Implementation of RSBY in Chhattisgarh, India: A Study of the Durg District", *Health Culture and Society* 2(1).

Public Health Foundation of India (PHFI) (2011). *A Critical Assessment of the Existing Health Insurance Models in India*. New Delhi. Accessed from *www.planningcommission.nic.in/reports/sereport/ser/ser_heal1305.pdf* (accessed on 10 April 2012).

Rajashekhar, D., Erlend Berg, Maitreesh Ghatak, R. Manjula and Sanchari Roy (2011). "Implementing Health Insurance: The Rollout of Rashtriya Swasthya Bima Yojana in Karnataka", *Economic and Political Weekly* XLVI(20): 56-63.

The Economic Times (2012). "Govt to Use RSBY Smart Cards to Deliver Life Insurance Cover to Poor". April 6. Accessed from *http://articles.economictimes.indiatimes.com/2012-04-06/news/31300207_1_rsby-scheme-health-insurance-scheme-rashtriya-swasthya-bima-yojana* (accessed on 20 July 2012).

Sethi, S. (2011). "Can Rashtriya Swasthya Bima Yojna Help Bridge the Quality Chasm?", *RSBY Working Paper*. Accessed from *www.idfresearch.org/pdf/RSBY_Hospital_quality_paper.pdf* (accessed on 15 May 2012).

Selvaraj, S. and A.K. Karan (2012). "Why Publicly-Financed Health Insurance Schemes are Ineffective in Providing Financial Risk Protection", *Economic & Political Weekly* XLVII(11).

Shahrawat, R. and K.D. Rao (2011). "Insured Yet Vulnerable: Out-of-pocket Payments and India's Poor", *Health Policy and Planning*: 1–9

Sun, C. (2010). "An Analysis of RSBY Enrolment Patterns: Preliminary Evidence and Lessons from the Early Experience", *RSBY Working Paper 2*. Accessed from *http://www.rsby.gov.in/Documents.aspx?ID=14* (accessed on 15 May 2012).

6

S. NANDI, M. NUNDY, V. PRASAD, K. KANUNGO, H. KHAN, S. HARIPRIYA, T. MISHRA and S. GARG

Implementing of RSBY in Chhattisgarh, India

A Study of the Durg District

Introduction

Providing financial protection against the cost of ill-health is stated as one of the fundamental objectives of health systems. This is in recognition of the fact that the health of individuals and that of the population is severely affected by the accelerating cost of health. The health system in India aims to provide universal coverage to the entire population of the country offering preventive as well as curative health services. The HSC (health sub-centre), PHC (primary health centre), CHC (community health centre) and district hospital play an important role in catering to the health care demands at various levels.[1] Nevertheless, India remains one of the countries with poor government spending towards health and a record of high out-of-pocket (OOP) expenses.

In India, the private sector accounts for more than 80 per cent of the total health care spending. In addition to private sector spending, the share of OOP expenditure in the country runs high which ultimately creates a financial burden on the households, pushing them increasingly towards poverty. According to Berman *et al.*,

1. A HSC covers a population of 5,000 in all areas except in tribal, hilly or desert areas where there is one HSC for a population of 3,000. A PHC covers a population of 30,000 in plain regions and 20,000 in hilly, tribal and difficult regions. CHC are 30-bed hospitals, with laboratory facilities, labour room and an operation theatre. These cater for the need of 0.12 million of population and 80,000 in hilly or tribal areas. As per the norms, a CHC provides referral back up to about 4 PHCs and 20 HSCs. A district hospital can be 100-bedded or even more with specialists for surgery; gynaecology; medicine and paediatrics. The diagnostics need to be sufficiently advanced for it to act as a referral centre.

(2010), more than 10 million households in India were pushed below the poverty line due to spiraling health care spending in 2004.

The burden of costs incurred for accessing medical care has increased over the last two decades. The latest data of the National Sample Survey (NSS) show that on average, households spend ₹ 295[2] for outpatient care and ₹ 7,116 for inpatient care. The NSS 61st Round, moreover, reports per capita expenditure in India to be ₹ 804 in the rural area and ₹ 958 in the urban area (Gupta, 2009). In India, health expenditure constitutes approximately 4.7 per cent of the total household outlay (Gupta, 2009). Likewise, the average expenditure for every hospitalisation has been estimated by Dilip and Duggal (2002) at ₹ 3,990. The analysis of the NSS 60th Round suggests that around 6.2 per cent of the total households (6.6% in the rural areas and 5% in the urban areas) fell below the poverty line as a result of health care spending in 2004. Approximately 1.3 per cent of the total households became BPL as a result of expenditure on inpatient care, while 4.9 per cent of households became so as a result of outpatient care (Berman *et al.*, 2010).

If the expenditure is disaggregated for private and public facilities, the expenditure is evidenced to be much higher in the former (Selvaraj and Karan, 2009). The National Rural Health Mission (NRHM) was launched by the government in 2005 in order to address what was described as the

> systemic flaws in the health system namely, the lack of a holistic approach; absence of linkages with collateral health determinants; gross shortage of infrastructure and human resources; lack of community ownership and accountability; non-integration of vertical disease control programs; inadequate responsiveness to community needs and lack of financial resources (Planning Commission, 2011a).

Within the paradigm of the NRHM, flexible financing was seen as one of the main approaches. This included risk pooling and demand side financing where money follows patients. However, even with the NRHM initiative and its emphasis on zero user fee services, many are still paying for health care services and OOP expenditure for most is a

2. One US dollar is equivalent to around ₹ 53.

common occurrence. To reduce OOP expenditures for health care and lessen a considerable financial burden on the poor, the Government of India (GoI) launched the national health insurance scheme Rashtriya Swasthya Bima Yojana (RSBY) in 2007 (Jain, 2010).

There have been various studies and commentaries on RSBY, especially in the last year, like by Narayana (2010), Rathi (2011), Das and Leino (2011), Palacois *et al.* (2011), and Reddy *et al.* (2011). These studies have looked at the implementation of RSBY, specifically issues of enrolment; utilisation; hospitalisation; empanelment of hospitals and OOP expenditure incurred by the beneficiaries.

In this study, we first introduce the readers to various components of RSBY design, such as enrolment; empanelment; utilisation and the cost of hospitalisation; OOP expenditure; transparency and governance; along with review of relevant literature. We then describe the study setting, measuring implementation of RSBY as given per secondary sources. The study objectives and methodology will then be introduced in detail. Subsequently, the findings related to the profile of the respondents, their level of awareness, experience of enrolment and of hospitalisation, as expenditure incurred are presented, allowing us to follow on with conclusive discussion.

Background to RSBY

In India, health insurance coverage has been limited to those in the organised sector and to those who can purchase insurance privately. There has been a growing concern over the last decade about the lack of social security measures and access possibilities for 90 per cent of the population who are in the unorganised sector. Evidence of growing inequities and lack of protection for majority of the population has consequently led to a renewed interest in health insurance as a way of providing financial protection during times of illness with some of the debates focusing on ways of providing financial protection to the poor so that they do not face indebtedness or slip off the health care radar.

There are very few health insurance schemes available for the unorganised sector. There have been several community-based insurance schemes mostly run by non-governmental organisations that are scattered with limited coverage. The past decade has witnessed governments introduce and experiment with various kinds of health financing strategies. We remember that a universal health insurance scheme (UHIS) was launched by the Ministry of Finance in 2003 but failed to take off due to weak design and lack of commitment from the state governments and governing principalities. Few experiments, moreover, such as the Rajiv Arogyashri Community Health Insurance Scheme (RACHI) which was launched for BPL families in Andhra Pradesh by the state government in 2007 seemed to gain the necessary momentum for successful implementation.

The debates on universal health insurance culminated with the launch of the RSBY in 2007. This was the first scheme to be launched nationally by the central government for the unorganised sector, targeting insurance cover for BPL households struck by major health trauma necessitating hospitalisation. Some of the major actors involved in designing the programme other than the Ministry of Labour included the GTZ,[3] the World Bank and the ILO.[4] RSBY did not replicate any existing insurance model but borrowed design features from several successful community-based insurance systems and nationalised health insurance systems of other countries such as Thailand, Canada, Germany and Chile. RSBY recognises the absence of health cover as a major insecurity amongst workers in the unorganised sector. It also acknowledges that expenditure relating to medical care and hospitalisation pushes people to seek recourse to inadequate, incompetent as well as incomplete treatment. Also taken into account by RSBY is the relative economic loss of work days, which affects both the livelihood of people as well as the economy (*www.rsby.in*). The definition for BPL is that which is prescribed by the Planning Commission for determining eligible BPL population in

3. Since 2007, GTZ (Deutsche Gesellschaft für Technische Zusammenarbeit GmbH) and then its successor organisation, the GIZ (Deutsche Gesellschaft für Internationale Zusammenarbeit, formed on 1 January 2011 through the merger of DED, GTZ and Inwent) have been supporting the Indian Government in designing and implementing the insurance model on behalf of the German Federal Ministry for Economic Cooperation and Development (BMZ). *http://www.giz.de/en/mediacenter/672.html*.

4. International Labour Organization.

state/districts.[5] The responsibility of verifying the eligibility of BPL families thus lies with the respective state governments that have to share the information with the insurance provider.

RSBY Design

The cost of running the scheme is divided between centralised and individual state governments, with the former bearing the major financing input (about 75%) for the scheme. The set figure was ₹ 30,000 as the cap for families, and the scheme was initiated to extend to five members of a family i.e., a unit (up to a unit of five): the household head, spouse, and up to three dependents and/or dependents would include children and/or parents of the head of the family. There was a set registration fee of ₹ 30 to be paid by the family. The scheme was established to cover pre- and post-hospitalisation expenses as well as pre-existing diseases.

RSBY is said to be rooted in a 'business model' in which "all the stakeholders as the service provider, the insurance company etc. have direct benefits, would take a proactive role in making this scheme successful" (Government of Chhattisgarh, 2008).[6] The state calls for a private or a public insurance company (licensed by the Insurance Regulatory Development Authority [IRDA]) for the bidding process.[7] Some of the requirements of the government on bids submitted include a benefit package in the form of a cashless facility where smart cards are issued to all qualifying persons. Likewise, the package seeks to facilitate engagement with local intermediaries (NGOs, etc.) for reaching out to BPL families and for assisting members to utilise health services after enrolment. A list of empanelled hospitals participating in the cashless arrangement is required to be submitted by the insurer to qualifying community members. The

5. BPL classification is calculated by the Planning Commission based on per capita consumption levels.
6. Mr Anil Swarup, Director General (Labour Welfare) at the State level workshop on RSBY held at Hotel Tulip, Raipur, on 15 October 2008.
7. The financial bid is an annual premium per enrolled household. Each contract is specified on the basis of an individual state district where the insurer agrees to set up an office in each district. While more than one insurer can operate in a particular state, only one insurer can do so in a single district at any given point in time (*http://rsby.in/*).

empanelled public or private hospitals must meet the basic minimum of government requirements, these being size and registration; and the set up of a special RSBY desk with a smart card reader and trained staff. Compensation for the insurer is based on the number of Smart cards issued; keeping in mind that the households covered are based on the number of smart cards issued, that is, one card per household where up to five members are able to avail facilities. The eligibility of BPL households for purposes of the scheme is provided by issuing smart cards to all beneficiary households.

Enrolment

As per the RSBY website, around 47 per cent of the BPL families are currently enrolled on the RSBY scheme nationwide (*www.rsby.in*). Tripura has the highest enrolment with 85 per cent, followed by Himachal Pradesh and Nagaland each recording 80 per cent. This nevertheless evidences the substantial gap in scheme accessibility for the Indian population which is largely rural and non-literate. Sun (2011) has studied enrolment patterns at village, household and individual levels using administrative data. The findings indicate that there are wide variations in enrolment rates across villages, districts, regions and demographic groups. Among the selected villages studied, 10.0 per cent of the villages were without enrolment and only in 2.5 per cent of the villages every eligible family was enrolled (Sun, 2011: 94). These variations may be linked to various factors such as discrepancies in BPL data which has not taken into account factors of birth, death, migration or marriage in the subsequent years after the BPL survey was conducted; poor power backup in the villages; low awareness among people about the scheme and enrolment schedule in their respective villages, etc. (Sun, 2011). Sun (2011: 95) further asserts that in terms of the insurer's behaviour there may be "geographic discrimination based on the cost of enrolment" or "healthier" villages may deliberately be selected for enrolment.

Similarly, Rathi (2011) in his evaluation of RSBY in Amravati, Maharashtra, found that the lack of information and late enrolment led to only 39 per cent enrolment in the district. The tribal blocks of the district which have the maximum number of poor households saw the least enrolment. The study further suggests that beneficiaries were concentrated in certain areas and villages.

Evidence was further found in the study by Sun (2011) that even within the enrolled families, five members of the family are not being enrolled under the RSBY scheme. According to the study, in 31.2 per cent of the families, less than five members were enrolled and only in 16.1 per cent of the families, all or up to five members of the family successfully became part of the scheme.

Narayana's (2010) study shows that RSBY in its third round covers only one-third (200) of the Indian districts, and out of these districts, more than 60 per cent belong to just four states: Uttar Pradesh (UP), Punjab, Haryana and Maharashtra. Apart from the above mentioned states and Chhattisgarh, Gujarat, Bihar and Kerala, hardly any enrolment has elsewhere been reported. The study also indicates huge enrolment variation within the states themselves, evidencing low enrolment in poorer districts.

It has been argued that any scheme which targets only BPL families risks leaving out a large number of actual poor communities due to exclusion errors in the BPL list itself. In Chhattisgarh, the government recognises 74 per cent of its population as poor and provides subsidised grain (Wadhwa, 2010). However, central government has fixed the percentage of BPL in the State at 46 per cent. Hence, there is a huge population of poor people who have not been even considered eligible for the RSBY scheme.

Empanelment

The government has empanelled public as well as private hospitals under the RSBY scheme giving families the choice of selection depending on their accessibility and convenience. According to a survey by Westat India School of Social Sciences (2010), by November 2010, nearly 5000 hospitals were empanelled under the RSBY scheme nationwide. The RSBY review study by Narayana (2010) indeed indicates that the percentage of public hospitals out of those empanelled in the sample states varies from 45.86 per cent in Kerala to 4.95 per cent in Haryana. The study signals that there is no public hospital empanelled under the RSBY scheme in Maharashtra.

Utilisation and Cost of Hospitalisation

Globally, various studies have been undertaken in order to determine utilisation and OOP expenditure under government insurance schemes. However in India as most of the programmes are new, such as the Arogyasri scheme in Andhra Pradesh and the Chief Minister Kalaignar's Insurance Scheme for Life Saving Treatments in Tamil Nadu, extensive data on these aspects remain scant if not unavailable. Research undertaken by Das and Leino (2011) indicates that although spreading awareness through the strategy of IEC (information, education and communication)[8] did not have a major impact on scheme enrolment, it did nevertheless have an impact on the utilisation rates of those who finally became enrolled. About 4.6 per cent of enrolled households that received the IEC (and 4% of households that received both the IEC and the household survey) have at least once used the services provided under the scheme (Das and Leino, 2011).

According to the study by Hou and Palacios (2011), utilisation rates vary largely across villages and districts. Their research reveals that districts served by three of the six insurance companies have higher utilisation rates than areas where two of the three are private insurers. It also found that the likelihood of RSBY scheme access depends on the number of people in the same village who have already utilised the benefits and the number of hospitals empanelled under the scheme in the area. The utilisation rate is also found to be concentrated to a select few empanelled hospitals in the district (Hou and Palacios, 2011).

8. IEC is the name given to the communication and education strategy introduced in India first in the 1960s to spread messages regarding family planning. This approach, focused on "driving home a few key messages," has since been criticised for being 'communicator (rather than receiver) centric' and has been discarded in favour of BCC or Behaviour Change Communication, which involves first understanding people's situations and influences, developing messages to respond to their concerns and using relevant and cultural specific communication processes and media to persuade them to increase knowledge and change risky behaviour and practices (Public Health Resource Network [PHRN] 2009a). However, unfortunately, often both nomenclatures are used interchangeably and without appreciating their differences.

According to the same study, by June 2010, there were approximately 80,000 hospitalisations per month. The average utilisation for all the villages studied stood at 4.3 per cent, and excluding villages where no hospitalisation was recorded, the rate rose to around 11.0 per cent. Only 26 per cent of the sampled villages experienced at least one hospitalisation under the RSBY scheme, with the annualised utilisation rate being 1.2 per cent for such villages (Hou and Palacios, 2011).

Narayana's (2010) findings show that the average hospitalisation rate per 1,000 persons over a scope of 365 days varies from 3.91 in Punjab to 24.78 in Gujarat. The study also reports the highest hospitalisation rate of 196.41 in the Dangs district of Gujarat and the lowest 0.07 in the Jalandhar district of Punjab. Among the selected states studied, the average cost of hospitalisation was highest for Punjab (₹6,606) and lowest for Kerala (₹3,101). Narayana suggests the low density of empanelled hospitals and the lower empanelment of the private hospitals in total as the probable factor for variation in district hospitalisation rates.

In a study assessing existing health insurance schemes, Reddy *et al.* (2011) find that the nationwide hospitalisation rate per 1,000 persons for 2009-10 stands at 20, taking into consideration those districts which have completed one year of the RSBY scheme. Assam, Goa and Chandigarh report the lowest hospitalisation rates of a mere 1 while Gujarat reports the highest at 42. The hospitalisation rate per 1,000 beneficiaries in other state-based insurance schemes is reported to be 5 in the Rajiv Arogyasri scheme; 4 in the Vajpayee Arogyasri and Kalaignar schemes and 22 in the Yesaswini scheme. This number is high (64) for private health insurance.

As per the study, the average nationwide hospital expenditure for RSBY is approximately ₹4,262 (Reddy *et al.*, 2011). The lowest expenses are reported in Tamil Nadu (₹886) and highest in Punjab (₹6,554). The claims ratio in this study is found to be 7.15 per cent, with Gujarat having the highest claims ratio of 14.53 per cent and Goa the lowest of 0.20 per cent (Reddy *et al.*, 2011).

Out-of-pocket Expenditure

A study on the implementation of RSBY in Delhi by Grover and Palacios (2011) found that of the patients interviewed, more than one-third had incurred OOP expenditure. The average claim amount was ₹3,700 and the additional average OOP expenditure was ₹1,690. More than two-thirds of OOP expenditure was due to prescribed medicines.

A study conducted to evaluate the Rajiv Arogyasri Community Health Insurance Scheme in Andhra Pradesh revealed that nearly 60 per cent of the beneficiaries of the scheme incurred OOP expenditure of approximately ₹3,600 mainly due to transport, medicine and pre-diagnostic investigations (Rao *et al.*, 2010).

Transparency and Governance

Narayana (2010) notes that there is very little information available in the public domain and emphasises the need for greater transparency and proactive disclosure about the details of admissions, the types of illnesses reported, and the procedures for a more comprehensive and cohesive analysis. Rathi (2011) in his evaluation of RSBY raises the issue of lack of a grievance redressal mechanism under the scheme and the lack of coordination among the various government departments in implementing the scheme.

Chhattisgarh

Chhattisgarh, a central Indian state, once a part of Madhya Pradesh, came into being in 2000. Chhattisgarh is the 10th largest state in India with an area of 135,191 km^2. With a total population of more than 25 million (Census, 2011), it is the 17th largest state of the country by population, having 18 districts[9] (recently further divided into 27 districts) with Raipur as its capital city.

9. In January 2012, the 18 districts were further divided into 27 districts. However, for the purpose of this chapter, we will continue with 18 districts as disaggregated data are not yet available for the new districts.

According to the National Family Health Survey (NFHS)-3[10] (2005-06) in Chhattisgarh, only 22 per cent of the households are situated in urban areas, with the remaining 78 per cent in rural areas. Of the total households, 30 per cent belong to scheduled tribes (STs), 14 per cent to scheduled castes (SCs) and 45 per cent to what is classified as other backward classes (OBC). Seventy-two per cent of the children aged 6-17 years attend school in the State, with 45 per cent of the females and 74 per cent of the males in the 15-49 age group being literate.

According to the Sample Registration Survey (SRS) 2007, the IMR (infant mortality rate) in Chhattisgarh stands at 59 and according to the SRS of 2004-05, MMR (maternal mortality rate) stood at 335.

Soon after it came into being in 2000, Chhattisgarh launched a series of health sector reforms in order to improve its public health system such as the Mitanin Programme,[11] a three-year medical course, and the formation of a cadre for rural and remote areas. The public health system in Chhattisgarh currently has around 4,741 health sub-centres (HSCs), 721 PHCs and 136 CHCs in addition to 18 district hospitals and 3 medical colleges in place.

According to Berman *et al.* (2010), in Chhattisgarh, around 5.0 per cent of the total households became poor (classified as BPL) due to spiraling health care costs in 2004. Of this, 0.5 per cent was due to inpatient care while 4.5 per cent was due to outpatient care in both rural and urban areas. Approximately 5.3 per cent of total household

---

10. The NFHS programme, initiated in the early 1990s, is one of the most important, exhaustive and credible sources of data on population, health and nutrition for India and its states and is led by the International Institute for Population Sciences (IIPS). The NFHS-3 (2005-06) is the third in the series of these national surveys, and was preceded by NFHS-1 in 1992-93 and NFHS-2 in 1998-99. This survey has been designed to provide estimates of critical indicators on family welfare, maternal and child health, and nutrition along with information on family life, education, safe injections, peri-natal mortality, adolescent reproductive health, high-risk sexual behaviour, tuberculosis, and malaria (IIPS and Macro International, 2007).

11. The Mitanin Programme is a government community health worker (CHW) programme in Chhattisgarh which aimed to facilitate people's access to health services within the village through community-organisation building and social mobilisation [European Union State Partnership Programme (EUSPP), 2011]. Lessons from the Mitanin progamme have helped in the formulation of a countrywide CHW programme called Accredited Social Health Activist (ASHA) steered by the NRHM.

expenditure (5.2% in the rural areas and 5.9% in the urban area) is allotted to health (Berman *et al.*, 2010).

RSBY in Chhattisgarh

In Chhattisgarh, RSBY was launched in June 2009 and Durg was the first district to be enrolled on the scheme. Chhattisgarh was one of the 15 states to have advertised RSBY in 2008. The distribution of smart cards began in 2009. A Memorandum of Understanding (MoU)) between the Centre and the state was signed by Director General and Labour Welfare and Health Secretary respectively; the former keeping in view that the scheme is to extend to cover all

Table 6.1

Status of Enrolment in Chhattisgarh up to 18 March 2011

No.	*Name of District**	*Year of Policy*	*Percentage Enrolled (No. of Families Enrolled/Total No. of BPL Families)*
1	Koriya	2	9
2	Dantewada	1	12
3	Raipur	2	26
4	Bastar	1	28
5	Kawardha	2	30
6	Durg**	2	37
7	Bilaspur**	2	45
8	Kanker	1	47
9	Mahasamund	2	52
10	Janjgir Champa	1	53
11	Raigarh	1	58
12	Korba	1	63
13	Dhamtari	1	65
14	Rajnandgaon**	2	69
15	Jashpur	1	87
16	Surguja**	2	119***
	Chhattisgarh		47

Note: *Data not available for Bijapur and Narayanpur;

**Total families based on website accessed on 6 August as data unavailable on 18 March 2011;

***Enrolment data uploaded on the website could be erroneous for both rounds of enrolment combined.

Source: *http://rsby.gov.in/Statewise.aspx?state=13* viewed on 18 March 2011.

workers in the unorganised sector under the Unorganised Workers Social Security Act.

The partners of the scheme are the government, the insurance company, the third party administrator (TPA) and the empanelled hospitals. As per the guidelines of the scheme, in Chhattisgarh, the insurers were selected through a bidding process. They in turn selected the TPA who is responsible for enrolment.

The RSBY scheme is currently functional in 16 out of 18 districts of Chhattisgarh. Only 47 per cent of all the total of 22,29,350 BPL families have been enrolled for the purpose of the scheme (Table 6.1). The enrolment rates vary across the districts with Dhamtari having the highest (65%) and Koriya the lowest (9%) rates (Table 6.1). The district of our study—Durg—has a total of 257,844 BPL families; out of which currently 95,670 families (37%) have been enrolled.

Table 6.2

Distribution of Empanelled Hospitals

No.	*District*	*Private*	*Public*
1	Bastar	4	18
2	Bijapur	0	0
3	Bilaspur	34	55
4	Dantewada	0	11
5	Dhamtari	6	5
6	Durg	20	39
7	Janjgir Champa	9	10
8	Jashpur	2	9
9	Kanker	0	10
10	Kawardha	6	4
11	Korba	13	10
12	Koriya	0	6
13	Mahasamund	5	5
14	Narayanpur	0	0
15	Raigarh	7	10
16	Raipur	91	36
17	Rajnandgaon	3	28
18	Surguja	7	71
	Chhattisgarh	207	327

Source: http://rsby.gov.in/Statewise.aspx?state=13, accessed on 18 March 2011.

A total of 207 private hospitals and 327 public hospitals have been empanelled under the scheme in Chhattisgarh (Table 6.2). It is significant that districts with difficulty of access to public facilities, for example the tribal districts of Dantewada, Kanker and Koriya, also do not have private providers who have been empanelled. While in Raipur District, where public facilities are relatively better than the above districts, 72 per cent of the hospitals empanelled are private hospitals. Thus, entry of the private sector in providing health services, fails to live up to the logic that in the absence or poor functioning of public health services, the private sector can effectively take up the task.

Table 6.3

Status of Utilisation as of March 2011

No.	*District*	*Enrolled BPL Families*	*Enrolled Population (Assuming Five Members Enrolled per Family)*	*Number of Hospitalisations*	*Percentage of Hospitalisations (No. of Cases Hospitalised/Total Enrolled Population)*
1	Kawardha	25372	126860	0	0
2	Koriya	5499	27495	0	0
3	Mahasam-und	62390	311950	0	0
4	Dantewada	9924	49620	44	0.09
5	Bilaspur	104626	523130	977	0.19
6	Rajnandgaon	78062	390310	858	0.22
7	Surguja	139192	695960	1617	0.23
8	Raipur	96516	482580	1663	0.34
9	Korba	72131	360655	1263	0.35
10	Kanker	27822	139110	511	0.37
11	Jashpur	57552	287760	1145	0.4
12	Janjgir Champa	68558	342790	1453	0.42
13	Bastar	43770	218850	1119	0.51
14	Raigarh	114695	573475	3505	0.61
15	Durg	95670	478350	4255	0.89
16	Dhamtari	37344	186720	1993	1.07
17	Chhattisgarh	1039123	5195615	20403	0.39

Source: http://rsby.gov.in/Statewise.aspx?state=13, accessed on 18 March 2011.

The utilisation status under the RSBY scheme, as per available data, is very low (Table 6.3). For Chhattisgarh, the percentage of hospitalisation is 0.39 per cent (20,403 cases). Here too the highest rate of hospitalisation is in Dhamtari (1.07%), followed by Durg (0.89%) (Table 6.3). At the time of the study, Durg had the highest percentage of hospitalisations.

The total cost of hospitalisation comes to approximately ₹95 million. The average cost of hospitalisation for the State is ₹4,650 (per case). The cost of hospitalisation for all the districts is detailed in Table 6.4. We find that the highest average cost of hospitalisation is in Raipur District (₹6,678), which incidentally also has the highest percentage of private hospitals empanelled (91%) (Table 6.2).

Table 6.4

Cost of Hospitalisation as of March 2011

S.No.	*Name of District**	*Number of Hospitalisations*	*Cost of Hospitalisation*	*Average Cost of Hospitalisation*
1	Raipur	1663	11106335	6678
2	Bilaspur	977	6193850	6340
3	Janjgir Champa	1453	7806662	5373
4	Dhamtari	1993	10405190	5221
5	Raigarh	3505	16801475	4794
6	Jashpur	1145	5487550	4793
7	Korba	1263	6035175	4778
8	Dantewada	44	210000	4773
9	Surguja	1617	6463405	3997
10	Kanker	511	2001925	3918
11	Durg	4255	15780228	3709
12	Bastar	1119	3895700	3481
13	Rajnandgaon	858	2678050	3121
	Chhattisgarh	20403	94865545	4650

Note: *No hospitalisations reported in Bijapur, Kawardha, Koriya, Mahasamund and Narayanpur Districts.

Source: *http://rsby.gov.in/Statewise.aspx?state=13*, accessed on 18 March 2011.

In 8 out of the 13 districts reporting hospitalisations, the average cost of hospitalisation is higher than the state average.

Figure 6.1

Cost of Hospitalisation as of March 2011

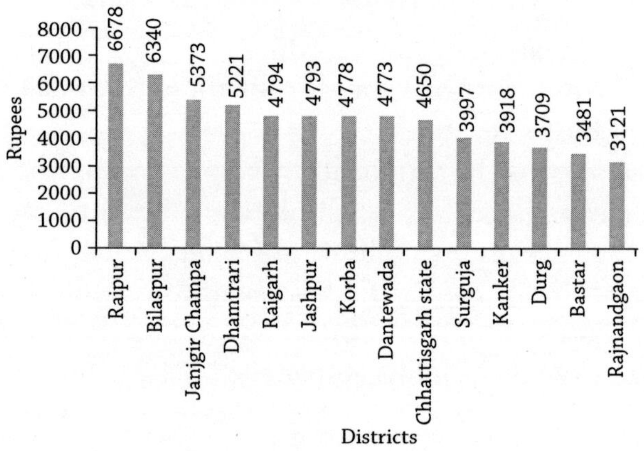

Note: *No hospitalisations reported in Bijapur, Kawardha, Koriya, Mahasamund and Narayanpur Districts.

Source: *http://rsby.gov.in/Statewise.aspx?state=13*, accessed on 18 March 2011.

The Durg District

The district of our study, Durg, had a total of 3,196 RSBY cases as of May 2010 (District Programme Management Unit [DPMU], 2010).[12] The majority of cases (82%) were from private hospitals while only 18 per cent were from public hospitals. The information accessed from the DPMU shows that compared to private hospitals, a higher percentage of cases from public hospitals were rejected by the Insurance company (Table 6.5).

Table 6.5

Details of RSBY Cases in Durg (as of May 2010)

Type of Facility	*No. of Cases*	*No. of Cases Rejected*	*% of Cases Rejected Out of Total Claimed*
Private	2633	252	10
Public	563	86	15
Total	3196	338	11

Source: DPMU, 2010.

12. Report given by the DPMU till May 2010.

Study Objectives and Methodology

The objective of our present study is to assess implementation and viability of the RSBY scheme in Chhattisgarh in order to identify RSBY policy gaps and programme inconsistencies in terms of enrolment, information dissemination, service utilisation, empanelment, availability of services in hospitals, transparency and the extent of OOP expenditure incurred by beneficiaries.

Secondary data were collected from the RSBY website (*http://rsby.gov.in/Statewise.aspx?state=13*), first accessed on April 2010 and then in March 2011. Data analysis was undertaken on equity aspects: enrolment, coverage, hospitalisation and empanelment.

District Selection

The district of Durg was selected as it had the highest percentage of hospitalisation under the scheme at the time (April 2010) and was also the first district to be enrolled.

Hospital Selection

Data were collected from two public hospitals and five private hospitals in the Durg District of Chhattisgarh. The selection of the hospitals was based on those with the highest number of cases served

Table 6.6

Details of Sample Hospitals

Name of Hospital	*Type*	*Number of Cases Under the RSBY Scheme as of May 10**	*No. of Respondents*
CHC Gunderdehi Villages: Khalari and Khamrod	Public	34	30
District Hospital	Public	518	20
Chandu Lal Hospital	Private	380	7
Gayatri Hospital	Private	328	18
Verama Hospital	Private	255	10
SS Hospital	Private	213	8
City Hospital	Private	74	7

Source: *: DPMU, Durg (2010).

under the RSBY scheme, as per data provided by the DPMU. Two public hospitals with the highest number of hospitalisations were selected for our study. The private hospitals were selected through convenience sampling from among those with the highest utilisation. Four days were spent at each hospital.

Sample Selection

A total of 52 people from public and 50 people from private hospitals were interviewed. This comprises 4 per cent of total hospitalised cases in the Durg District and 2 per cent of total cases in Chhattisgarh (as of 30 April 2010). The study covered two out of the total of 16 empanelled public hospitals and 5 out of the total 10 empanelled private district hospitals (Table 6.6).

Primary data were gathered through patient interviews availing the RSBY scheme both from public and private health facilities and was collected during May and June 2010. The selection was done as per patients available on the particular days on which researchers visited the hospitals. For the CHC, initially, exit interviews of the patients were conducted with an alternative methodology thereafter being adopted owing to the hospital ceasing to admit patients under the RSBY scheme for a week in June as the RSBY supervisor had taken leave. The team therefore identified two villages with the highest RSBY beneficiaries through discussions with CHC staff and visited those villages (Khalari and Kamrod). In the villages, the research team took the help of the ASHAs, known as Mitanins in Chhattisgarh, to identify beneficiaries who had availed RSBY in the CHC over the last two months. The beneficiaries were then interviewed.

An attempt was made to cover 10 cases (10 such patients who had utilised the RSBY scheme) per hospital. The selection of the patients was based on convenience both in the hospitals and the villages.

Interview Method

The study was undertaken using a structured questionnaire in the form of exit interviews. The questionnaire used was first pilot tested on five patients.

Information regarding awareness of the scheme and enrolment procedure was gleaned by assessing sources of available information on RSBY; public awareness of the breadth of coverage; knowledge of treatment covered; enrolment sites and respective locales; public awareness of costs incurred in reaching enrolment sites and venues; awareness of the registration fee incurred; and knowledge of the validity of the smart card and its renewal procedure.

To elicit information on hospital procedures, our questionnaire focused on the illness/symptoms that prompted patients to seek health assistance; the hospital approached for treatment; the mode of travel to hospital; the assistance received at the RSBY counter; the diagnostic test undertaken; and knowledge of credits blocked from the card following hospitalisation and those remaining to be utilised.

Information was also gathered on access to medicine; expenditures incurred through OOP expenses during hospitalisation (whether these be for medicines or tips). Our questionnaire sought to elicit responses on the procedures undergone by the patients and whether they had been duly informed of diagnostic procedures and the respective costing incurred.

Findings from Primary Study

Demographic Profile(s)

Our study collated responses from a sample of 50 beneficiaries who were admitted and treated at public institutions and 52 at private sector hospitals.

Fifty-six per cent (57) of the respondents were female and 44 per cent (45) male (Table 6.7). There were 25 male and 27 female respondents from public hospitals with 20 male and 30 female respondents from private hospitals. Most of the cases were aged between 19 and 59 years.

Among the respondents, around one-fourth were not literate. Although the average number of family members of the respondents was 5, significantly, 37 per cent had more than five members in their family. Seventy-one per cent of respondents in public hospitals and 34 per cent respondents in private hospitals were from rural areas.

Table 6.7

Distribution by Demographic Characteristics (n=102)

Particulars		*Percentage*	*Number*
Sex	Female	56	(57)
	Male	44	(45)
Age	Below 5 years	1	(1)
	5-18 years	11	(11)
	19-59 years	75	(76)
	60 years and above	14	(14)
Caste	ST	27	(28)
	SC	21	(21)
	OBC	9	(9)
	General	43	(44)
Marital status	Unmarried	25	(25)
	Married	67	(68)
	Widowed	8	(8)
	Divorced	1	(1)
Level of schooling	Primary	58	(59)
	Secondary	19	(19)
	No education	24	(24)
Number of family members	5 and below	63	(64)
	Above 5	37	(38)

Awareness of RSBY and Respective Enrolment Procedures

The success of any programme depends on the awareness levels of the people it is meant to engage with. A significant number of the respondents came to know of the scheme through *panchayat*/ward members, this sooner being understood as word-of-mouth.[13] None of the respondents affirmed that they had received RSBY information through government health practitioners.

13. *Panchayat* members are elected representatives who are part of the Panchayat Raj System, a system of local self-governance involving village councils in India.

Figure 6.2

Persons Giving Information about RSBY

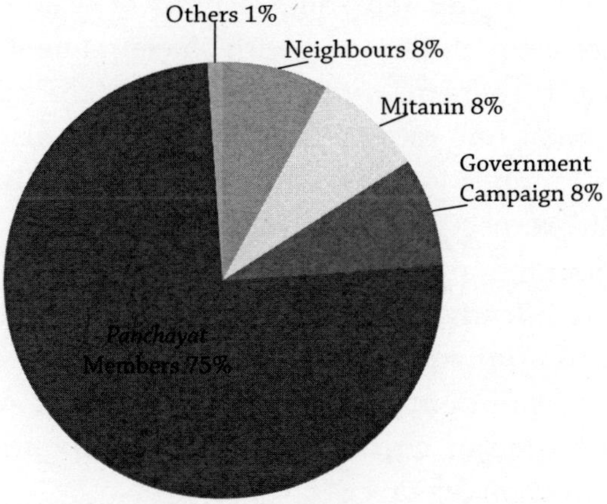

When inquired as to the purposes of the smart card, what it stood for and how it could be utilised, majority of the patients simply understood it to be along the lines of 'health insurance' or 'free medical services.' Patients, however, remained unaware of the details of scheme entitlement and usage. Although awareness regarding the amount available under the scheme was high, knowledge of the smart Card validity period and the qualifying number of family members to be enrolled was scant (Table 6.8).

Table 6.8

RSBY Awareness

Parameters	*Aware (%)*	*Unaware (%)*
Awareness regarding scheme purpose	84	16
Awareness regarding amount covered under scheme	90	10
Awareness regarding the smart card validity period	25	75
Awareness regarding the number of family members who could be covered under scheme	31	69

Enrolment onto the RSBY scheme is undertaken by the TPA. The procedure includes taking thumbprints and photographs of the family members to be covered and a deposit of ₹ 30 per family. The smart card is prepared on the spot, with the enrolment team handing over the card to the beneficiary before it leaves the village. The card becomes functional one month later. The TPA is also supposed to provide all the families with an RSBY brochure listing empanelled hospitals and the respective scheme entitlements.

Our study found that at the time of enrolment, both thumbprints and photos were effectively taken of all the respondents. However, in 99 per cent of studied cases, the RSBY brochure was not given; consequently, respondents were without the list of empanelled hospitals at the time of enrolment. All the respondents reported paying the registration fee of ₹ 30.

In 92 per cent of cases, family members accompanied the head of the family. In six out of the remaining eight families, only the head of the family was enrolled. Although more than one-third of the families had more than five family members, an average of four family members per family was enrolled onto the scheme (Figure 6.3).

Figure 6.3

Number of Family Members

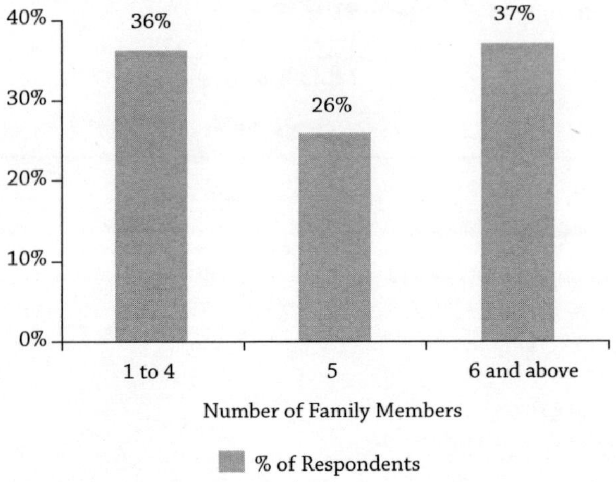

The average number of days taken to receive the smart card was 29. Only 4 per cent of the respondents received the card on the same day, whereas for the rest, the time taken to receive their cards ranged from 2 to an excess of 150 days (Figure 6.4). The guideline, however, states that the card is supposed to be given to the beneficiary on the day of enrolment as the RSBY entitlement starts from that day itself. A delay in receiving the card thus can logically signal a delay in accessing health care and assistance.

Figure 6.4

Waiting Time for the Smart Card

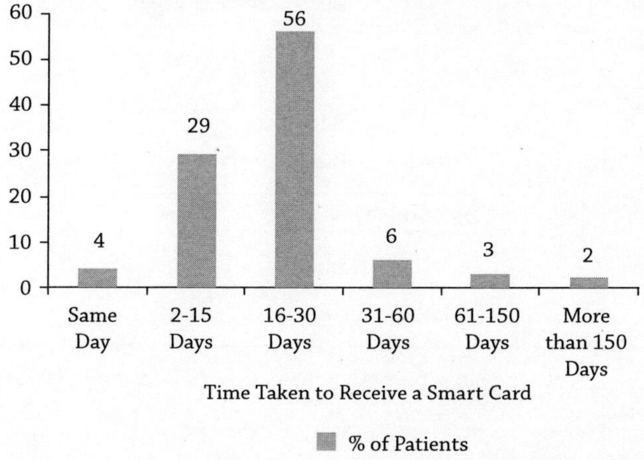

While 77 per cent of the respondents had visited local schools for enrolment, 17 per cent were enrolled in their *Panchayat*, with 4 percent in the community hall. None of the respondents had to spend any money in reaching enrolment venues.

Hospital Selection

The respondents were asked as to who had suggested services/ treatment from the respective hospitals: 24 per cent stated neighbours; 21 per cent stated the Mitanin (ASHA in Chhattisgarh) as the source of information; 16 per cent said that either relatives or the TPA who enrolled them were the source of information; 9 per cent stated that health staff had recommended access services from a particular hospital.

Figure 6.5

Persons Suggesting a Private/Public Facility

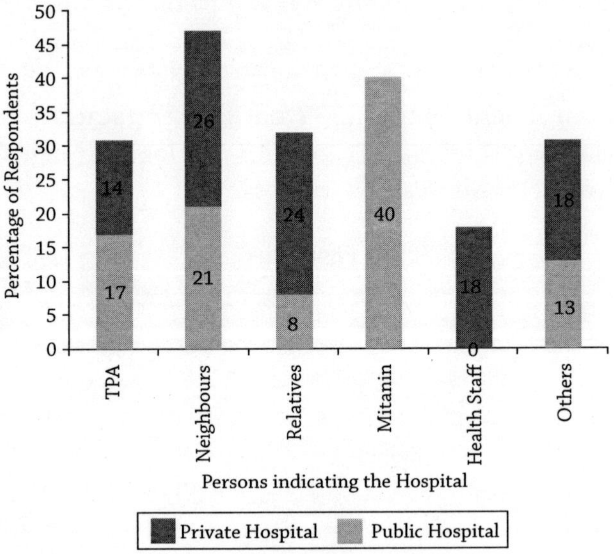

Table 6.9

Reasons for Accessing Care

Reason for Hospital Visit/Admission	*Male % (n=45)*	*Female % (n=57)*	*Total % (n=102)*
Weakness	29	33	31
Fever	22	12	17
Surgery	4	5	5
Abdominal pain	4	12	9
Accidents	11	2	6
ENT	4	5	5
Diarrhaea/dysentery/vomiting	2	7	5
Delivery	0	7	4
Paralysis	4	0	2
AIDS	2	0	1
Fracture	7	0	3
Uterus problems	0	12	7
Others	9	4	6

If we compare the respondents at the public facility and the private facility, it was found that 40 per cent of the patients at former were informed by the Mitanin (ASHA) to access services from that particular facility, while the health staff suggested private hospitals (Figure 6.5).

In order to reach the hospital, 60 per cent of the respondents required public transport, while 37 per cent opted for private transport and 3 per cent walked. Ninety-nine out of 102 patients used some form of transport and the average amount spent on such was ₹ 57.

Reasons for which Medical Care was Sought

In terms of the reasons for which medical care and assistance was sought, 33 per cent said they did so because of weakness, 18 per cent stated fever, 13 per cent said they came for surgery, 10 per cent due to abdominal pain and 9 per cent because of accidents. Other than this, 5 per cent sought treatment for diarrhoea/dysentery/vomiting, 3 per cent for undergoing C-Section, 2 per cent had paralysis and one person had come to seek treatment for AIDS.

Hospital Experience

At the hospital, 97 per cent said that their card was seen first and verified by the RSBY registration counter (RRC). For the remaining 3 per cent, the card was seen at the OPD (outpatient department) counter. According to registration norms and RSBY protocol, it is mandatory for the hospital to issue verification slips which then need to be presented to the attending clinician. In 70 per cent of the cases, no verification slips were issued.

Patients were mostly unaware of Smart Card verification. In 70 per cent of cases, the doctor had requested the card be verified. Others requesting verifications were attendants (13%); receptionists (11%); nurses (3%); and data entry operators (1%).

The average waiting time for verification was 14 minutes. The average waiting time for medical consultation and assistance was 9 minutes, and the average time of consultation was 11 minutes.

Diagnostic Facilities and Medicines

Diagnostic tests were indicated for 63 per cent of patients with 17 per cent not requiring such procedure. Forty per cent of the patients in the public hospitals and 86 per cent in the private hospitals were asked to get diagnostic tests done. Of the patients who were prescribed tests, nearly all had to get their blood tested (Figure 6.6). Other tests were those of urine, stool, X-ray; sonography, electrocardiography (ECG), and a computed tomography (CT) Scan. Fourteen per cent of the respondents were unaware of the nature and intent of the tests requested (Figure 6.6).

Figure 6.6

Diagnostic Tests (n=64)

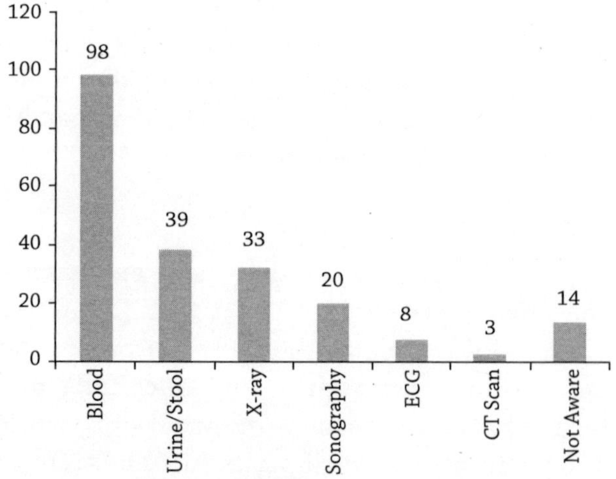

In 75 per cent of cases, the requisite tests were undertaken on site at the hospital itself, with 19 per cent of cases being undertaken outside in private laboratories (Figure 6.7).

Figure 6.7

Site of Diagnostic Test

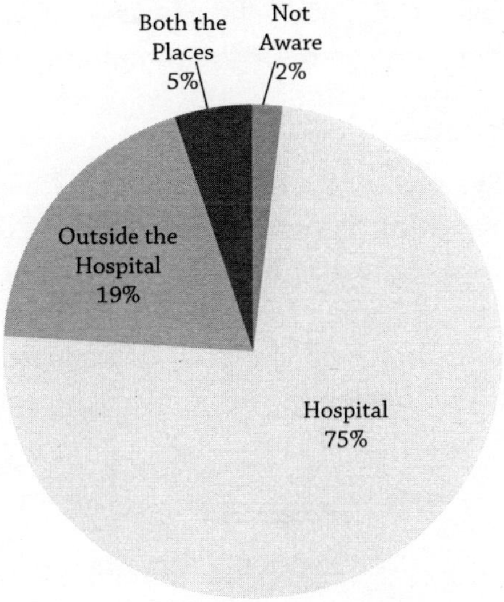

For 60 per cent of the respondents, medicines were available in the hospital, while for 38 per cent of patients, medicines had to be purchased from private pharmacies (Figure 6.8).

Figure 6.8

Availability of Medicines

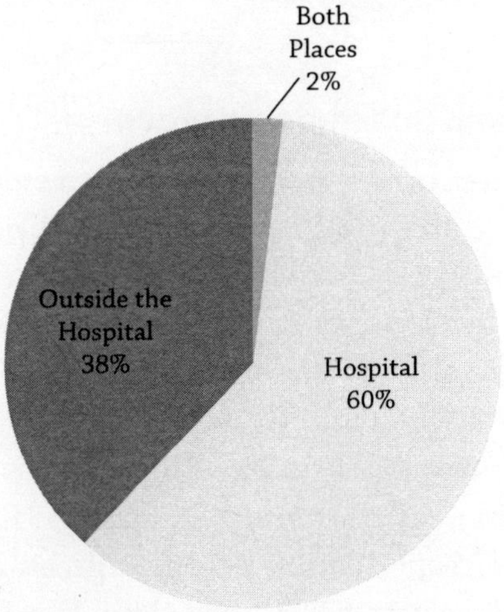

Among the respondents who purchased medicines off-site, the respective pharmacy was indicated by the RSBY nodal person in 50 per cent of cases; in 45 per cent of cases, it was the attending clinician, while others indicated for the remaining 5 per cent of cases.

Hospitalisation Period

The average days of hospitalisation recorded were five. Although all patients were recorded as being hospitalised, 26 (25%) said that they were never hospitalised. Six of these patients were from the private hospitals and 20 were from public sector hospitals. Of the persons hospitalised, most of them were admitted to the general ward (Figure 6.9). Furthermore, 50 per cent of patients required a form of procedure during their stay.

Figure 6.9

Details of Hospitalisation

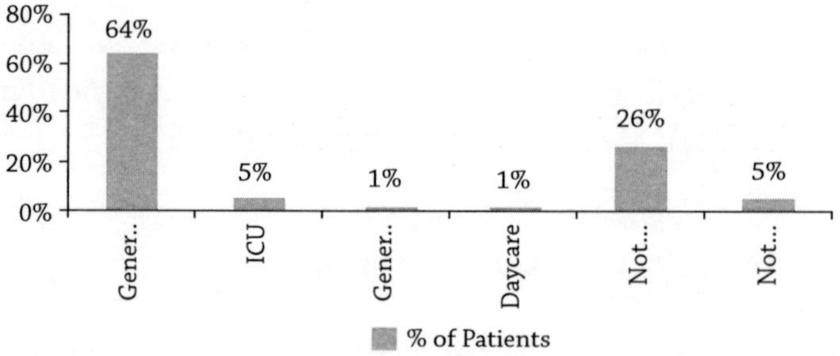

RSBY Entitlement and Scheme Utilisation

Among the patients, 77 per cent had previously utilised the RSBY scheme. Out of the total respondents, 63 per cent were aware of the amount of money blocked by the hospital for the current hospitalisation, while 37 per cent were unaware of how much money had been blocked by the hospital or indeed how many credits remain on the smart card.

The average amount blocked was ₹6,622. This was higher in the private hospitals than in the public hospitals (Figure 6.10). Fifty-nine per cent of the respondents were not given any receipt for the amount blocked from their RSBY card. Ninety-nine per cent of the respondents received transport charges of ₹100 by the hospital as per RSBY norms.

Figure 6.10

Average Amount Blocked from the Smart Card

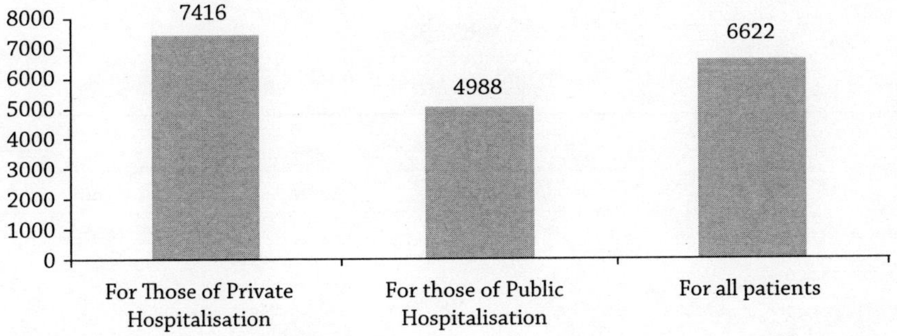

Out-of-pocket Expenditure

Of all the respondents, 37 per cent incurred OOP expenditure. Fifty-eight per cent who went to private hospitals incurred OOP costs as compared to the 17 per cent of public hospital respondents.

The average amount of OOP expenditure was ₹686. In the public hospitals, the average amount the beneficiaries had to spend was ₹309, while in the private hospitals it stood at ₹1,079 (Figure 6.11).

Figure 6.11

Average Out-of-pocket Expenditure Incurred

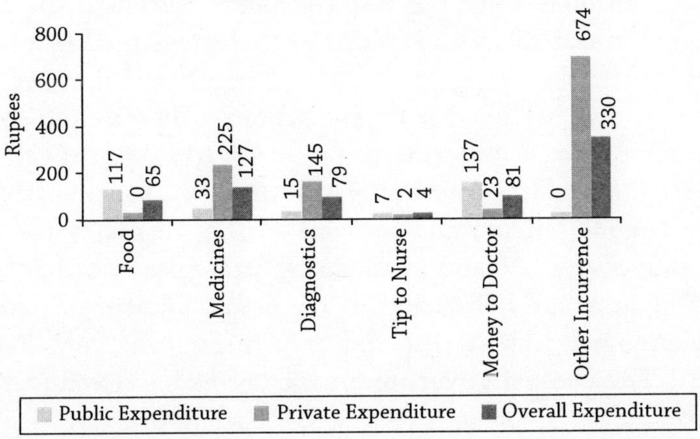

Nineteen per cent of the expenditure was on medicines; 12 per cent as money given to doctor; 11 per cent in diagnostics; 9 per cent on food; and one had to tip the nurse (Table 6.10). Forty-eight per cent of the respondents were not aware of the purpose for which all the money had been solicited.

Table 6.10

Head-wise Percentage for Out-of-pocket Expenditure

	% to Total Spent		
Expenditure Head	*Public*	*Private*	*Total*
Food	38	1	9
Medicines	11	21	19
Diagnostics	5	13	11
Tip to Nurse	2	0	1
Money to Doctor	44	2	12
Others	-	63	48
	100	100	100

Discussion

Low Coverage of Poor Families in the State

Enrolment and coverage of the poor: Analysis of secondary data shows that less than half of BPL families in the district and the State have been enrolled onto the RSBY scheme. Although the scope of our study did not reach to exploring the factors for low enrolment in Durg, such a low rate signals that a significant number of poor families are still excluded from the scheme. This finding correlates with other research undertaken by Sun (2011), Rathi (2011) and Narayana (2010). It also emphasises the need for identifying the reasons for low enrolment, as well as the necessity for stricter monitoring of the TPA and formulating strategies in order to ensure that the poorest are not excluded. The actual number of poor in the state, moreover, may be resolved only through universal coverage of RSBY. The central government has agreed to expand RSBY to all workers under the National Rural Employment Guarantee Act (NREGA),[14] yet this still remains to be implemented.

Number of family members covered: The scheme stipulates that a maximum of five members may be covered in a family. In the study, 37 per cent of the respondents had more than five family members, hence they had to make a decision as to who to include and who to exclude. This finding corresponds to data collated by Sun (2011) showing that in a society with such widespread discrimination against women, young girls, disabled persons and the elderly, there is a danger of the most vulnerable members of the family being left out.

RSBY Awareness

Our study shows that *panchayat* members have played an important part in introducing the scheme to the people, while in rural areas, Mitanins also proved instrumental in facilitating scheme access. Nevertheless, community awareness regarding the details of the scheme was low. A brochure along with the list of hospitals was to be distributed at the time of enrolment as a scheme protocol, but our research shows that this simply was not the case. Consequently, the respondents saw RSBY as a health insurance scheme; they were unaware of pre- and post-hospitalisation coverage, diagnostic, transportation, follow-up and food expenses. Likewise, respondents knew little if not nothing about scheme choices and entitlements, empanelled hospitals or the money blocked for each spell in the hospital. This demonstrates that necessary and adequate information was not shared with people during enrolment or afterwards, and that there is a weakness in the community dissemination of crucial scheme information.

For ensuring successful implementation and optimum utilisation of any health insurance scheme (and indeed in order to optimise community access), beneficiaries need to have knowledge and information about the scheme, its workings as well as its limitations. The strategy of IEC has shown to have a positive role in increasing utilisation trends (Das and Leino, 2011). The lack of knowledge

14. The NREGA provides a minimum of 100 days of work annually for all rural families.

and information not only prevents utilisation of health insurance benefits but may also lead to malpractice by the hospitals. Therefore in order to empower beneficiaries, spreading awareness through the use of both written and oral media is necessary. The possible ways of spreading scheme awareness could be through community wall writings and billboards, radio/TV programme similarly, and the use of local folk media such as street theatre, songs, etc. Orientation about the scheme to key persons in the village or to *panchayat* members could also prove equally useful.

Enrolment Procedures

Our study indicates that families are at risk to losing out on precious time to utilise the card. The smart card has to be given to the beneficiary before the enrolment team leaves the village; however, this has not been the case for there have been delays in card issuance.

The enrolment procedure itself did not cause inconvenience incurring little financial burden other than ₹30 per registering family. Requisite scheme information such as the list of empanelled hospitals, an RSBY brochure or key phone numbers of the respective officials was lacking. For a number of families, only the head of the family received scheme coverage as the rest of the family members did not attend the enrolment session. Such patterns and tendencies indicate a failure to follow-up and ensure coverage for all family members at a later date.

Empanelled Institutions

In Chhattisgarh, 61 per cent of the empanelled facilities are public. This is a positive trend considering that nationally, 70 per cent of the empanelled hospitals are from the private sector (Narayana, 2010).

The process of empanelment is, however, without transparency and remains independent of the public domain for hospitals with highly inadequate facilities were also clustered and empanelled under the scheme. The empanelment of private facilities had also been propagated in order to increase access to health services in areas where the public health system was not functioning well. Yet when

we look at secondary data, it is evident that this is not the case. Districts with a weak public health system simply do not have the adequate number of private facilities to fulfil the demands of access and coverage. For example, although tribal districts represent nearly half the number of total districts in Chhattisgarh, RSBY has not been initiated in two of the districts and in the remaining districts, only 6 per cent of the total private hospitals have been empanelled. Forty-four per cent of the total private hospitals empanelled in the state are in Raipur, where the state capital is situated, which at the same time has functional public health facilities.

None of the private hospitals have been empanelled in remote districts such as Kanker, Koriya and Dantewada; thus no additional facilities have emerged through RSBY.

Low Utilisation Rates

The rate of utilisation may be analysed in two ways. One would be to assess the hospitalisation rate for a particular population and to what extent RSBY is able to cover demand. The second analysis would be to see how healthy the claims ratio is.

In terms of hospitalisations, secondary data show an abysmally low rate of hospitalisations, a mere 0.39 per cent in fact. The need is much higher for, as we find in some states, scheme utilisation has reached more than 20 per cent (Reddy *et al.*, 2011; Narayana, 2010).

In addition to low utilisation trends, the study also reveals that around one-fourth of the patients who were shown to be hospitalised were not actually hospitalised. This points to the risk of fraud and malpractice by empanelled hospitals who artificially increase the utilisation rate for the ends of financial return. More stringent checks, protocols and balances need to be put into place to reduce the tendency of scheme fraudulence.

The low rate of hospitalisation in Chhattisgarh further signals that in proportion to the premium paid by the Government to the insurance companies, the claims have been miniscule. Literature reveals that the claims ratio of a well-functioning insurance scheme has to be around 80 per cent (PHRN, 2009b). Studies show that nationally the claims ratio in RSBY is low (Reddy *et al.*, 2011). Past evidence suggests that the response of targeted groups to insurance schemes may be disappointing. This however relates to informational and administrative impediments rather than a deliberate choice or risky behaviour.

Hospitalisation Costs under the RSBY Scheme

The Chhattisgarh study shows that the cost of hospitalisation is significantly higher than in other Indian states (Reddy *et al.*, 2011; Narayana, 2010). As the amount does not include the OOP expenditure incurred by the patients, it may be concluded that the actual expenditure per hospitalisation is much higher. This, therefore, signals the increasing cost of care which may be artificially created.

Out-of-pocket Expenditure

Our study evidences that more than one-third of the beneficiaries had to incur OOP expenditure and this was more the case in private hospitals. Such findings correlate with the study in Delhi by Grover and Palacios (2011). In private hospitals, maximum expenditure is on medicines and diagnostics. This too mirrors the findings of Grover and Palacios (2011). In the public hospital, most of the expenditure was on food and money given, whether or not in kind, to the doctor. Such high expenditure in this 'cashless' scheme is of serious concern as the RSBY initiative was seen as a model to remove such health care costs.

Our study thus points to high expenditure despite the ethos of the scheme. RSBY was initiated with the logic of cushioning the poorer section of the population. This philosophy nevertheless seems to be compromised as expenditure is still incurred and continues to be high.

Issues of Transparency

Transparency of the scheme seems to be highly questionable considering that many patients were unaware of the amount deducted from the smart card and receipts were not given to beneficiaries after the treatment. The hospitals too are not informed of the reasons for the rejection of claims; while in the study, we found that a significant number (11%) of cases had been rejected. During data collection, details of hospitalisations and hospital-wise data were not made available. A detailed and meaningful analysis can only be possible through a higher level of disclosure (Narayana, 2010).

Conclusion

Currently, there have been many discussions and debates on the model for universal health care coverage in India. We have seen the participation of government, committees set up for health planning and policy; academicians; civil society and health activists regarding the design and universalisation of health care; and within it, the role of insurance and the private sector. An article in the Lancet series on universal health care in India signalled the move towards universalising health coverage through insurance schemes akin to the RSBY scheme, as well as the active participation of the private sector (Shiva Kumar *et al.,* 2011). However, the High Level Expert Group (HLEG) on universal health care established by the Planning Commission, taking cognisance of the shortcomings of insurance and experiences worldwide, has rejected the insurance model (HLEG, 2011). The HLEG has instead recommended a tax-based system for universalising health care coverage where the government rather than an external agency like the TPA buys the services of private providers.

In order to understand the scope and impact of RSBY, investigative and planning effort needs to be placed within the wider health policy and strategy of India. RSBY came on the heels of the government's flagship programme, the NRHM which started in 2005 and which continues to provide the framework wherein health programmes are being designed. NRHM is seen as a comprehensive health care model aimed at improving access to quality health services in rural areas through decentralisation, flexible financing, improved management capacity and community participation. RSBY on the other hand uses an insurance route with the high involvement of the private sector. There thus seems to be a lack of symmetry between NRHM and RSBY.

The objectives of the RSBY scheme are nevertheless pertinent to the current health scenario in India. RSBY has the capability of protecting the poor from high hospitalisation expenses thereby preventing such a proportion of the population from further impoverishment. For the people utilising RSBY, the services available seem to have expanded with the choice of accessing private health care providers. However, there are a number of challenges and weaknesses in the scheme as illustrated by our study.

One main issue is precisely population coverage which remains very low in India. In contrast, we find that many countries such as Canada, Germany and Thailand have achieved very high nationwide coverage through their health insurance schemes. RSBY is supposed to cover only a third of India's population, specifically those living below the poverty line. Yet it is a well-known and documented reality that there are serious problems in definition, estimation and identification of the poor in BPL surveys.

Another set of issues are in the implementation of RSBY at all levels: from selection of the insurance companies and TPAs, enrolling of the BPL population, mechanisms for informing the population about the scheme, empanelment of hospitals, to the patients' hospital visits. At all levels, there are concerns relating to accountability and transparency. This has been largely discussed in our study where we evidence major gaps and the lack of structural cohesion. The slow pace of enrolment combined with the lack of information and ambiguity about the scheme amongst the beneficiaries prevents them from seeking medical care under the scheme. This results in a low claims ratio benefiting the insurance company at the cost of public funds. OOP expenses for the poor continue to be very high despite the utilisation of RSBY and hospitals have been found to selectively deny and filter certain services to the poor. In order to improve the implementation of RSBY, more information needs to be made available to the beneficiaries. Involvement of the community both in implementation and monitoring is critical to ensure that the poor are actually benefited from such insurance programmes (Desai, 2009). In the case of RSBY, in-built mechanisms for such community processes are absent.

Many of the above concerns have been addressed by countries such as Germany, Thailand, Philippines, Canada and Chile through setting up strong regulatory frameworks and empowering the beneficiary. While RSBY can take a lead from these countries, it is also important to understand the differences of context. RSBY is meant for people in the unorganised/informal sector in India who are in fact highly scattered, disunited, impoverished, disempowered and have low bargaining power. This scheme pits the poor unorganised sector in India against the powerful private for-profit agencies like insurance companies, TPAs and hospitals, which, as experience has shown can hardly be expected to work in favour of BPL families. For many other developing countries, the challenges have remained in terms of health equity, poor health infrastructure, problems of geographical access and unhealthy competition between public and private providers. The challenge, both structural and ethical, is great.

Furthermore, there are serious doubts as to whether the health outcomes at the population level would improve through such a scheme as RSBY—it simply does not cover the range of primary health care services (curative, preventive and promotive) required for such an impact. There remains a fundamental design-flaw, namely the lack of access to free and quality primary health care and the low coverage of catastrophic illnesses striking the poor. While today in India, the availability of free health care for primary illnesses and low health status of the rural poor are serious concerns, experiences worldwide have shown that insurance schemes may lead to an artificial increase in costs and inferior health outcomes.

Our study therefore throws serious doubts on whether RSBY is actually making free and quality health care more accessible to the poor. At a time when RSBY is being showcased by some as the confident step towards universal health care coverage, the question remains whether it is not simpler to invest in strengthening the public health system in providing services and building their capacities to regulate private providers, rather than bringing in complex mechanisms like RSBY. Are such insurance schemes the only way forward to providing financial security to the poor against spiralling health care costs especially when its impact on health outcomes is contentious?

References

Ahuja, Rajeev and Alka Narang Alka (2005). "Emerging Trends in Health Insurance for Low-Income Groups", *Economic and Political Weekly* 40(38): 4151-57.

Berman, P., R. Ahuja and L. Bhandari (2010). "The Impoverishing Effect of Health Care Payments in India: New Methodology and Findings", *Economic and Political Weekly* 45(16).

Carrin, G. and C. James (2005). "Social Health Insurance: Key Factors Affecting the Transition towards Universal Coverage", *International Social Security Review* 58(1). Geneva: World Health Organization.

Chongsuvivatwong, V., K.H. Phua, M.T. Yap, N.S. Pocock, J.H. Hashim, R. Chhem, S.A. Wilopo and A.D. Lopez (2011). "Health and Health-care Systems in Southeast Asia: Diversity and Transitions", *Lancet*, 377(9763): 429-37.

Das, Jishnu and Jessica Leino (2011). "Evaluating the RSBY: Lessons from an Experimental Information Campaign." *Economic and Political Weekly* 46(32).

Desai, Sapna (2009). "Keeping the 'Health' in Health Insurance", *Economic and Political Weekly* 44(38): 18-21.

Dilip, T.R. and Ravi Duggal (2002). "Incidence of Non-Fatal Health Outcomes and Debt in Urban India", Draft Paper prepared for *Urban Research Symposium*. December 9-11. Washington DC: The World Bank.

Duggal, Ravi (2005). "The Out-of-pocket Burden of Health Care", *InfoChange News and Features*. June. *http://infochangeindia.org/20050612402/Agenda/Access-Denied/The-out-of-pocket-burden-of-health care.html* (accessed on 1 December 2010)

European Union State Partnership Programme (EUSPP) (2011). *Evaluation of the Community Health Volunteer (Mitanin) Programme*. Raipur: Department of Health, Chhattisgarh.

Government of Chhattisgarh (2008). *Minutes of the State Level Workshop on RSBY.* October 15. Raipur. health. *cg.gov.in/.../RSBY%20-%20State%20workshop%20oct%202008.pdf* (accessed on 11 December 2010).

Grover, Seema and Robert Palacios (2011). "The First Two Years of RSBY in Delhi" (Chapter 6), in R. Palacios, J. Das and C. Sun (eds.) (2011), *India's Health Insurance Scheme for the Poor: Evidence from the Early Experience of the Rashtriya Swasthya Bima Yojana*. Centre for Policy Research.

Gupta, Indrani (2009). *Out-of-pocket Expenditures and Poverty: Estimates from NSS 61st Round*. Delhi: Institute of Economic Growth.

Hatcher, Gordon H. (1978). "Canadian Approaches to Health Policy Decisions-National Health Insurance", *American Journal of Public Health* 68(9): 881-89.

High Level Expert Group (HLEG) (2011). *High Level Expert Group Report on Universal Health Coverage for India*. Submitted to the Planning Commission of India, New Delhi. *http://planningcommission.nic.in/reports/genrep/rep_uhc2111.pdf*

Hou, Xiaohui and Robert Palacios (2011). "Hospitalization Patterns in RSBY: Preliminary Evidence from the MIS" (Chapter 5), in R. Palacios, J. Das and C. Sun (eds.) (2011), *India's Health Insurance Scheme for the Poor: Evidence from the Early Experience of the Rashtriya Swasthya Bima Yojana*. Centre for Policy Research.

International Institute for Population Sciences (IIPS) and Macro International (2007). *National Family Health Survey (NFHS-3), 2005–06: India*. Volume I. Mumbai: IIPS.

International Labour Organisation (2008). "Extension of Social Security to BPL Workers: Rashtrya Swasthya Bima Yojana: Planning Situation", *Discussion Paper Series*. *http://www.ilo.org/public/english/region/asro/bangkok/events/sis/download/paper7.pdf*

Jain, Nishant (2010). *56 Million Steps towards Universal Coverage: RSBY Health Insurance for the Poor in India.* (GTZ) GmbH Eschborn.

Lawn, J.E. (2008). "Alma Ata: Rebirth and Revision 4-30 years after Alma Ata—Has Primary Health Worked in Countries?" *The Lancet* 372(9642): 950-61.

Mavalankar, Dileep and Rames Bhat (2000). *Health Insurance in India: Opportunities, Challenges and Concerns.* Ahmedabad: Indian Institute of Management.

Ministry of Health and Family Welfare (2005). *Financing and Delivery of Health Care Services in India. Background Papers* of the National Commission on Macroeconomics and Health.

Narayana, D. (2010). "Review of the Rashtriya Swasthya Bima Yojana", *Economic and Political Weekly* 45(29): 13-18.

NSS (2006). *Morbidity, Health Care and Condition of the Aged: NSS 60th Round.* New Delhi: Ministry of Statistics and Programme Implementation, Government of India.

Office of the Registrar General and Census Commissioner (2011). "Provisional Population Totals: Chhattisgarh", Census of India 2011. *http://censusindia.gov.in*

Palacios, R., J. Das and C. Sun (eds.) (2011). *India's Health Insurance Scheme for the Poor: Evidence from the Early Experience of the Rashtriya Swasthya Bima Yojana.* New Delhi: Centre for Policy Research.

Planning Commission (2011a). *WG1: Progress and Performance of National Rural Health Mission (NRHM) and suggestions. In Report of the Working Group on National Rural Health Mission (NRHM) for the Twelfth Five Year Plan (2012-2017).* New Delhi: Government of India.

———. (2011b). *Press Note on Poverty Estimates. http://www.planningcommission.nic.in/reports/genrep/Press_pov_27Jan11.pdf* (accessed on 24 March 2011).

Public Health Resource Network (PHRN) (2009a). *Behavior Change Communication and Training for Health.* Book 5. New Delhi: Public Health Resource Network.

———. (2009b). *Engaging with the Private Sector*, Book 12. New Delhi: Public Health Resource Network.

———. (2009c). *Introduction to Public Health System.* Book 1. New Delhi: Public Health Resource Network.

Rao, M. (2010). "Health for All' and Neoliberal Globalisation: An Indian Rope trick", in L. Panitch and C. Leys (eds.) (2010), *Socialist Register 2010: Morbid Symptoms: Health under Capitalism.* New Delhi: LeftWord Books.

Rao M., S. Kadam and T.N. Sathyanarayana (2010). "A Rapid Evaluation of the Rajiv Aarogyasri Community Health Insurance Scheme-Andhra Pradesh", Abstract for EPHP. *http://www.ephp.in/wp-content/uploads/2011/01/A-Rapid-Evaluation-of-the-Rajiv-Aarogyasri-Community-Health-Insurance-Scheme.pdf* (accessed on 5 February 2011).

Rathi, Prateek (2011). *Evaluation of Rashtriya Swasthya Bima Yojana, a Health Insurance Scheme for Below Poverty Line People in Amravati.* Bangalore: IIM.

Reddy, K. Srinath, Sakthivel Selvaraj, K.D. Rao, M. Chokshi, P. Kumar, V. Arora, S. Bhokare and I. Ganguly (2011). *A Critical Assessment of the Existing Health Insurance Models in India.* Public Health Foundation of India.

Results for Development Institute (n.d.). *Moving toward Universal Health Coverage: Rashtriya Swasthya Bima Yojana (RSBY) India: A Case Study. http://jlw.drupalgardens.com/sites/jlw.drupalgardens.com/files/RSBY%20Case%20Study%202-24-10%20FINAL.pdf*

Selvaraj, S. and A. Karan (2009). "Deepening Health Insecurity in India: Evidence from National Sample Surveys since 1980s", *Economic and Political Weekly* 44(40): 55-60.

Shiva Kumar, A.K., L.C. Chen, M. Choudhury, S. Ganju, V. Mahajan, A. Sinha and A. Sen (2011). "Financing Health Care for All: Challenges and Opportunities", *Lancet* 377(9766): 668-79.

Soors, W., N. Devadasan, V. Durairaj and B. Criel (2010). "Community Health Insurance and Universal Coverage: Multiple Paths, Many Rivers to Cross", *Background Paper* 48. World Health Report.

Sun, Changqing (2011). "An Analysis of RSBY Enrolment Patterns: Preliminary Evidence and Lessons from the Early Experience" (Chapter 4), in R. Palacios, J. Das and C. Sun (eds.) (2011), *India's Health Insurance Scheme for the Poor: Evidence from the Early Experience of the Rashtriya Swasthya Bima Yojana.* Centre for Policy Research.

V. Tangcharoensathien, W. Patcharanarumol, Por Ir, S.M. Aljunid, A.G. Mukti, K. Akkhavong, E. Banzon, D.B. Huong, H. Thabrany and A. Mills (2011). "Health Financing Reforms in Southeast Asia: Challenges in Achieving Universal Coverage", *Lancet* 377(9768): 863-73.

Vellakkal, S., S. Juyal and A. Mehdi (2010). "Health Care Delivery and Stakeholder's Satisfaction under Social Health Insurance Schemes in India: An Evaluation of Central Government Health Scheme (CGHS) and Ex servicemen Contributory Health Scheme (ECHS)", *Working Paper* 252. New Delhi: Indian Council for Research on International Economic Relations.

Wadhwa, D.P. (2010). *Central Vigilance Committee on Public Distribution System Report on the State of Chhattisgarh.* Justice D.P. Wadhwa Committee. New Delhi.

Westat India Social Sciences (2010). *RSBY Beneficiary Experience Survey, 2010* (accessed on 2 June 2009).

Websites

Health Indicators of Chhattisgarh, Demography. *http://cghealth.nic.in*

Rashtriya Swasthya Bima Yojana, Guidelines. *www.rsby.in.* Accessed on 13 March 2010.

Rashtriya Swasthya Bima Yojana, Overview. *www.rsby.in.* Accessed on 5 December 2011.

Acknowledgements: We are grateful to Dr K.R. Antony, Former Director, State Health Resource Centre, Chhattisgarh, and Dr K. Madan Gopal, Former CEO, State Nodal Agency RSBY, Chhattisgarh, for their valuable feedback on this study. We wish to acknowledge the Foundation for Inclusive Growth-Centre for Child Health and Nutrition (IFIG-CCHN) which has provided financial support to PHRN. We are grateful for the support and cooperation extended by district officials, hospitals, their staff and members of the Mitanin programme. Most of all we are grateful to the respondents who shared their experiences with us, enabling us to build and decipher this complex and tense picture.

This paper was originally published in 2012. Full reference: Nandi, S., M. Nundy, V. Prasad, K. Kanungo, H. Khan, S. Haripriya, T.Mishra and S. Garg (2012). "The Implementation of RSBY Scheme in Chhattisgharh, India", Health, Culture and Society 2(1). Available on *http://hcs.pitt.edu/ojs/index.php/hcs/article/view/61/99*

7

C.J. JISHA

The Comprehensive Health Insurance Scheme (CHIS) in Kerala

An Exploratory Study in Kollam District

Introduction

Tracing the early history of health insurance programme, the first national health insurance programme was implemented in Germany in 1893 by Bismarck, the Chancellor of Germany. Under this programme, the state provided compulsory insurance coverage through contributive deduction at source (salary) for every state employee (Borowitz and Atun, 2006). The beneficiaries had the option of choosing between private and public service provider. Those who could not pay the premium, the state-run scheme took them in their fold. This model later came to be known as the Social Health Insurance. By putting together a social security system, including medical insurance for industrial workers, Bismarck was able to appease the workers.

National health plans were established in different countries around early 1900s: in England it was established in the year 1911, 1914 in Sweden, and 1930 was the year when it was established in France. All these plans were mainly for the salaried people who would be looked after by the employer or the government and most often, the dependents were left out of the purview of benefits. Around the later 1980s, almost every developed country had a health insurance coverage plans for its citizens.

In India, the formal sector employees receive assured social insurance type of benefits, which include the central government as well as the state government employees. The employees have dedicated hospitals where they can seek treatment and also seek referrals to tertiary care hospitals. The employees can claim reimbursements for the treatment sought and also buy medicine supplies with their entitlements. The Employees State Insurance (ESI) and Maternity Benefits Acts cover only select group of individuals and their families. The ESI Act of 1948 is a social insurance scheme covering those employed in public sector undertakings and any industry that uses power and employs more than 10 people. It provides four types of benefits namely, medical, sickness, maternity and work injury. It places a limit on the coverage of people based on their income levels. However, these income levels are revised in accordance with the market rates.

The Central Government Health Scheme (CGHS) was introduced in the year 1954 and provides treatment facilities under all systems of medicine, and treatment is available to the currently in service members as well as those who have retired from service. The service of CGHS is available mostly in big towns. Most of the major towns in India are covered under the scheme. The central government employees who are entitled to seek treatment are provided with a unique identification card, which must be used in all transactions.

The ESI and the CGHS are two schemes run by the government for their employees in regular employment, and it is quite different from those that are offered by the private and other NGO (non-governmental organisation) providers. The private insurance market has seen a spurt since the opening up of the insurance sector for foreign players in 1999. Since then, a number of private and foreign players have launched schemes for individuals and for groups. The insurance market is partially regulated.

The present study is about the centrally sponsored health insurance scheme which was adapted and modified in Kerala to be called the Comprehensive Health Insurance Scheme (CHIS). The presence of an old tradition of welfare funds targeted at certain sections of the society presents a picture of the state which has been adept at evolving new schemes and also adapting centrally run schemes for benefit of the population in the state.

The inequalities in access, affordability and availability of health care are important determinants in determining health of the population (Shiva Kumar *et al.*, 2010). The determining factors are in turn affected by other factors like government policy, law of the land and will of the administrators. The increasing levels of inequality and the resultant lack of access to health care has prompted the intervention of the state in a number of ways, in financing and provisioning of services. These include targeted interventions, cash transfers, provisioning of services in poorer districts and mass campaigns (Sen, 2011).

The Idea of Health Insurance

The idea of health insurance is considered as an alternative as well as a paradigm shift in health policy. This entailed a shift in the role of the state in financing, provisioning and as administrator of services to that of primarily financing and regulation (Escobar *et al.*, 2011). Within countries, the poorest households seem to suffer the most because of their lack of ability to access and afford health care. They have limited resources to purchase services from the private providers, and this leads them to seek services from the state-funded system, which might be short-staffed and not well maintained. Policy makers in several countries, low to middle income, are trying to argue for the inclusion of health insurance as an alternative method to scale up the efforts to improve health outcomes in countries (Escobar *et al.*, 2011).

The development of policy initiatives in order to help those below the poverty line seek medical attention has taken different forms. The Rashtriya Swasthya Bima Yojana (RSBY) allows for the provision of free treatment in public hospitals and subsidised treatment in private hospitals with the smart card technology to claim benefits up to a preset limit. The idea of the RSBY is premised on a PPP (public-private partnership) model which includes an embedded business model to help the insurer, the service provider as well as the patient (Harlankar, 2010). The inherent business model of RSBY made it attractive for the insurers; the provision of 75:25 financing was also attractive for the state governments.

The employees in the formal sector, those associated with the organised sector had their own system of safety nets through the CGHS and the ESI for the central government employees and for state government employees respectively.

The political context of RSBY traces its origin to the first term of the United Progressive Alliance (UPA) which came up with the Common Minimum Programme (CMP). The scheme though announced in the year 2007 by the then Prime Minister Manmohan Singh, the actual roll-out started in the year 2008 (Rajsekhar *et al.*, 2011).

Goals and Features of RSBY

The RSBY, a national health insurance scheme, was introduced in various states in the year 2008 in a phased manner, aiming to cover the entire nation by the year 2012-13. It had been initiated by the central government and launched by the Ministry of Labour to provide health insurance for workers belonging to unorganised sector who fall in the BPL category. This scheme was part of the Unorganised Workers Social Security Act of 2008. This scheme was envisioned to include the workers of the unorganised sector and their families. The scheme has an upper limit of ₹30,000 for a family of five, which can be claimed in a year, in case of illness and which also extends to diseases that are pre-existing in nature except certain basic exceptions.

Implementation

Finance and the Roll-out of the Scheme

The financing of the scheme has been divided between the central and the state governments in the ratio of 75:25, wherein the central government provides 75 per cent of the premium amount and the rest of the premium is to be provided by the state government. In Jammu & Kashmir (J&K) and the Northeastern states, the amount of contribution of the central government is 90 per cent and the rest is to be paid by the state government.[1] The state government is

1. Official RSBY documents.

also entrusted with the responsibility of collecting the registration amount from the users at the time of enrolment. The contribution of the users varies from ₹30 for the BPL population to the entire premium amount in case of APL (above poverty line) families.

An amount of ₹30,000 is the upper limit for all claims of hospitalisation expenses; different procedures are priced as well as administered differently. The patient is required to carry the card while seeking treatment, and for registration at the point of service. The holder of the card is made to get his thumb read on the biometric reader and briefly mention his illness to the RSBY kiosk operator. The kiosk operator has to later mark the patient as a registered case and allot a package according to the description of the patient's ailment and later has to get all the prescriptions marked for being reimbursed or charged from the card. The scheme also has provisions for supply of medicines at the cost of the empanelled hospitals during the period of hospitalisation and up to 5 days after discharge from the hospitals. It is the right of the patients to receive equal treatment on par with other categories of patients in empanelled hospitals.

Comprehensive Health Insurance Scheme

In Kerala, the RSBY and CHIS are jointly implemented by the Labour and Rehabilitation Department, Health and Family Welfare Department, and the Local Self-government Department. The Labour and Rehabilitation Department is the nodal agency which administers the scheme. A separate agency, Comprehensive Health Insurance Agency of Kerala (CHIAK), was entrusted with the implementation of the scheme. During the first year of implementation, 135 hospitals in the public sector, and 165 in the private sector, including hospitals in the cooperative sector were part of the scheme. In the government sector, all the hospitals at the level of CHC (community health centres) and above were empanelled. In addition, the five medical colleges from different districts were also empanelled. The insurer for the first and the second year was United India Insurance Company.

The state also expressed its desire to extend the scheme to the rest of the population by opening up the ceiling on premium payments, and allowing the full payment of premium, which worked out to be

₹506, plus ₹60 for the smart card. By this time, most of the other states had implemented the basic version of the scheme and had rolled out pilot projects in select districts of the state. The government in Kerala had decided to expand the scheme to encompass the whole state and to run in all 14 districts of the state.

The state government put out notifications inviting competitive bids for the insurance partner for scheme. During the first year of the scheme, the insurer was United India Insurance that managed to keep the contract for the continuing years as well. Most of the ground work has been entrusted to the third party administrator (TPA) (MD India Healthcare Services) from Pune. The responsibility of this TPA included the deployment of field staff for installation and upkeep of the software and electronic interface of programme. The TPA also works as a mediator between the Insurer and the service provider, helping with the manual claim of insurance claims of the hospitals for the treatment that was offered. Most of the other procedural formalities involved in the working of the scheme were also undertaken by the TPA. The TPA was chosen after a process of tender. The company also retained their contract from 2008 to 2011 and has expanded the range of services offered.

The Transition from RSBY to CHIS in Kerala

The RSBY scheme was implemented in Kerala on 2 October 2008. The scheme was to be launched in two districts in Kerala namely, Kollam and Alappuzha in the initial year. The central government had agreed to let the state go ahead and implement the scheme in all 14 districts in the state during the first year. Two districts were selected by the state government for the initial round of implementation.[2] The state government of Kerala through its Health and Family Welfare Department issued orders on 17 August 2008 with regard to the implementation of RSBY for the unorganised sector workers who were in the BPL category and CHIS for the non-BPL category under the Labour Department.

2. Government of Kerala , G.O No. 17571/J2/07/LBR.

The RSBY scheme was modified as the CHIS in Kerala. Unlike the RSBY that covered only those in BPL category, CHIS expanded its coverage to include APL families as well. This scheme was to include all those people who were classified as being below poverty line according to the Planning Commission's guidelines and also those who were eligible under the list prepared by the state government. The implementation of the scheme required that the state government should take efforts to verify eligibility of the BPL workers and their families and then enlist them into the scheme. The state government had to ensure that the requisite number of human resources required for the formation of a nodal agency, as envisioned by the directives of the central government and the state government's Labour Welfare Department, be adhered to. The nodal agency in Kerala was called CHIAK.

Under CHIS, existing diseases were also covered and there was an extensive list of rates for different surgical procedures to be followed by the empanelled hospitals. The scheme also offered a personal accident insurance claim in case of an accident to the card holder. The accident insurance coverage is for an amount of ₹25,000 per annum.

The CHIS in Kerala had been conceptualised as a cashless insurance scheme, where the beneficiary, the owner of a smart card, can seek treatments from empanelled hospitals which include the CHCs, ESI hospitals, district hospitals and willing private hospitals.

The empanelment of private hospitals was based on several conditions with regard to their capacity of their infrastructure and manpower. The requirements for empanelment of the private providers were overseen by the TPA as well as the insurance agency. It was also required by the agency CHIAK that insurance agency should employ field staff to look into various issues that might come up during the roll-out of the scheme. This included conducting technical classes for the use of the software as well as the process of manual claim submission in case of software failure.

The cashless system could be implemented because of tie-ups with medical stores and other diagnostic service providers who provide services to the beneficiaries. The diagnostic service providers can be private players who agreed to provide these services at subsidised rates. At the public hospitals, these tie-ups would mean subsidised medicines from medical fair price shops within the vicinity of the hospital. The same provision in private hospitals meant that the (hospitals) provide medicines and the required care during the inpatient care and also provide medicines for five days after being discharged.

If enrolment and utilisation of a scheme are any measures to go by, then surely the RSBY scheme has managed to gather a lot of interest and also a lot of beneficiaries. Most of the beneficiaries also reported the ease in the operation of the scheme as a feature that had attracted their attention and also the cashless feature as the one that had motivated them to seek treatment in private as well as public hospitals. Increasing number of workers has mentioned the ease of claims and the seemingly easy methods of uptake of the services at even private hospitals as one of the features that had attracted a lot of interest and also savings considering the increasing costs of medical expenses as well as increasing amounts of incidental indebtedness caused by catastrophic medical expenses.

Increase in the medical expenses coupled with the unavailability of services in the rural areas also makes this RSBY scheme a very popular one in the rural areas in most of the states.

Objectives of the Study

The present study was undertaken to look at the CHIS scheme in Kollam district, which is the broad objective here. The scheme under study has been operating in the district since 2 October 2008. The specific objectives of the study are to:

- To understand the socio-political context of CHIS.
- To study the eligibility, design and implementation of CHIS in Kollam.
- To study the experience of beneficiaries of different providers. The different providers being:
  (i) Public sector provider.
  (ii) Private (Not for profit).
  (iii) Private (for profit).

Taking into consideration the various objectives, the tools used are interview methods with key informants and also semi-structured interviews to talk and gather information about the scheme from people who have been closely associated with the scheme.

To meet the first objective i.e., to study the socio-political context of CHIS, the researcher interviewed officials involved in the design and implementation of the programme from the state government as well as the nodal agency, which was entrusted with the duties of acting on the scheme and working out the implementation and empanelment details. In order to get a complete picture, an effort was also made to talk to the TPA, who were involved in the grass-roots level implementation of the scheme.

In order to meet the second objective i.e., to study eligibility, design and implementation of the scheme in Kollam, the researcher interviewed the district nodal officers and the PROs (public relations officers) appointed by the state government, who were working at the different empanelled hospitals in the district. The local nodal officer of the RSBY scheme was also interviewed for details about the scheme and its status in the district.

The specific objective of getting to know the experience of the beneficiaries was met by interviewing the patients who had been seeking care at the specific hospitals. In one instance, the researcher had visited the residence of the beneficiary to gather details about the experience of the patient and his view about the scheme.

Brief Background About the Study Area

The field area chosen for fieldwork is Kollam district in Kerala. The area is well known for its cashew and coir industries, also known as the part of erstwhile Travancore state. This area is noted for the important role it played in the formation of workers' movement in the coir industry. However over the last several decades, the coir industry was experiencing a decline in production and export for a variety of reasons of infrastructural and other issues. Apart from coir, the other major industry is cashew processing.

Health Care

The town has a large number of private as well as public hospitals. While the main district hospital is situated right at the centre of the town, the mother and child hospital is also situated near the main district hospital. The area is also dominated by caste- and religion-specific clusters of medical service providers.

The oldest among them being the Sankers Hospital, situated very close to the city centre and is well known for various specialty departments.

Some other hospitals that are situated in and around the district hospitals have been around for more than 30 years and attract large number of patients. The district hospital has seen expansion and increase in number of patients over the years, and this has led to vigorous expansion in the infrastructure and the materials. The number of hospitals with modern facilities has seen a constant increase; there are new medical colleges that have been established even in small towns and villages.

Data Collection

The data collection for the study included 24 hospitals as listed on the website of the RSBY/CHIS as being empanelled in the scheme. The maximum number of hospitals were private hospitals whose number came to 14 and the remaining 10 were government hospitals. The data collection was done during November 2010 to April 2011.

The study was exploratory in nature and looked at the scheme from the provider as well as the beneficiary perspective using descriptive methods. The area of study was Kollam district in Kerala. The data collection included visits to all the empanelled hospitals and the interview of all people involved with the scheme in the hospital. The insurance provider—United India Insurance Company—was also approached to gather knowledge about the scheme, and their responses to the reported problems of high claim ratio as reported in the press. The beneficiary perspective was looked at by interviewing patients who had sought treatment at the hospital and by visiting their homes after getting to know their details while they were exiting the hospital. The cooperation of the service provider was sought by talking to the hospital administration; in private hospitals by written requests to the administration and the people who were involved in manning the kiosks, the hospital administration staff and the owners.

The source of data for the scheme and its implementation was collected from the official website of CHIAK, and articles on the scheme were collected from vernacular press and also from independent research that has been done on this scheme.

The universe of study was RSBY/CHIS empanelled hospitals in Kollam district, including both the public and private service providers. The hospitals empanelled under the scheme ranged from single owner hospitals and nursing homes to private medical colleges.

The method of selecting the three different types of hospitals was purposive, keeping in mind their ownership pattern and also the bed strength which was close to 50. Thus, the selection of three hospitals which provided CHIS services included a private for-profit hospital, a private not-for-profit hospital and a public sector provider.

The hospitals are based in Kollam district and are situated in different settings, and attract large number of both RSBY and non-RSBY patients. While the number of private hospital which continued to work under the scheme as of April 2011 were 10, there were also 10 public hospitals.

The data collection was done among the patients who were currently seeking treatment and were about to get discharged. The data collection was done using interview method, where the beneficiary was asked questions about his/her experience at the hospital and about the services and the changes if any that they wished to see.

During the second stage of data collection done during March to April 2011, in-depth interview method applied for with the service providers and their representatives as well as the patients.

Major Findings

The Rationale of CHIS

The CHIS in Kerala had been worked out as a scheme, where everybody irrespective of their status could get themselves treated at private as well as public hospitals. The condition that people in the APL category could also apply was what made the scheme a comprehensive one. The inclusion of the people from the state's BPL list also ensured that nobody was left out of the safety net; this meant that the state was willing to let private and public hospitals that were ready to empanel themselves provide treatment at subsidised rates.

The comprehensiveness of the scheme is defined at the attempt to include all the willing population who were interested in getting themselves enrolled in the scheme, and it assured that along with BPL beneficiaries, some APL beneficiaries had also applied for the cards and sought services of the hospitals in their respective districts.

Scope of the CHIS

The number of beneficiaries in Kollam according to official records as of 19 November 2010 (time of initial fieldwork), the data for Kollam district shows that there are almost 19,151 APL patients and 184,160 BPL patients. The claim settlement for the district of Kerala according to the same record stands at ₹1088.50 lakh. The major amount of which went to the private sector which gathered around ₹778.15 lakh, followed by the public sector which gathered ₹310.35 lakh. The numbers presented above depict a picture of preference for the private sector in Kollam district. This trend has been noticed in Thiruvananthapuram, Calicut, Kannur and Kasargod districts.

Public-Private Mix in Provisioning

The study focused on the implementation, working and roll-out of the CHIS in Kollam district. From the data gathered, it was noticed that there were marked differences in the ways in which the scheme was implemented over Kerala. In certain districts the empanelment of private hospitals was noticed to be way higher than the public hospitals. The case of Kollam was no different. The number of private hospitals exceeded public hospitals with 14 in the private sector and 10 in the public sector.

Who Benefits from Public Insurance Schemes?

Several important questions arise and these include: 'Who benefits from the Scheme?' Who stands to gain by this model? Is the TPA playing the role of a middle man? Are the private hospitals the main beneficiaries? Does the target population stand to gain any benefit? Is it beneficial for the government in trying to provide services to people who fall out of the group that can afford to buy health care? The answer to the above questions lies in analysing the trends in implementation of the scheme.

In this whole procedure, the private hospital stands to gain the exchequer's money through the model of health care delivery which places emphasis on production of receipts as an indicator of service delivered. The unconventional method of allowing private hospitals to compete with the public hospitals using the same scheme has produced mixed results. Taking the case of Kollam district, the initial enthusiasm had died down by the time the scheme had rolled into its second year. The scheme had also become very popular leading to a large number of people seeking services of the different hospitals, and an increasing clamour for empanelment by private hospitals.

The tendency of the poor to seek health care at private institutions is once again reinforced by the findings that given a choice, people preferred to use the private sector more than the public sector. The preference and also the feeling among people being treated in public hospitals is that they are being neglected and not treated at all. The image of a private provider was that of being clean, providing round the clock service, being well staffed and manned at all times of the day or night. The patient armed with a smart card had a choice of seeking medical attention from the public or private sector. Majority of them seemed to prefer using the private over the public sector. This is also reflected in the revenue earned by private hospitals from the public insurance scheme.

Misuses in the Public Insurance Scheme

The misuse of public insurance scheme was observed at several levels. For example, the provision of ₹100 as travelling allowance for every visit to a maximum of ten trips a year was also subverted at the main district hospital. The staff associated with the scheme would ask patients to sign a receipt for the travel allowance of ₹100 but they received only ₹95. The remaining amount was ostensibly deducted for the paperwork involved at the kiosk. The receipt would mention the entire amount while the cash in hand received by the beneficiary would only amount to ₹95. According to the medical superintendent, this practice of deducting money was legitimate as the kiosk operator was doing all the paperwork and was entitled to some remuneration for the work done.

The subversion of funds and the methods of claiming money for fake hospitalisations and other 'adjustments' had been draining the state's coffers; but unless a sturdy mechanism is evolved, this would continue. The patient who would be in a hurry to get himself/herself discharged may not notice that there has been a deduction from the amount due to him/her and would be unknowingly signing on the receipt.

The scheme that was envisaged to be cashless has ceased to be so. But as the scheme progressed, the provision of other ancillary services like scanning and other procedures was slowly sub-contracted to private operators because of lack of these services at the public hospitals. The most jarring of these instances was the case of scanning services being referred to a private provider and patients being asked to purchase medicines due to the short supply at the taluka hospital's attached medical store. Here, the patient was forced to buy medicines from the private provider.

The provision of services by the private providers is extremely variable in terms of quality. A private hospital that was empanelled by the CHIS at Oachira had poor infrastructure and the operation theatre was in a bad condition. Despite this, the hospital performed minor operations and procedures as outpatient services that helped augmenting the hospital's resources. These procedures would also not place a demand on the beds but still earn them money on account of the procedures performed. The condition of such hospitals had not been looked at during the time of empanelment.

The inclusion of the 'for profit' sector raises a larger question of whether the insurance scheme is diverting public subsidies for strengthening the market. The utilisation pattern of those covered by CHIS suggests that since a large percentage are choosing private hospitals for their treatment, public subsidies are largely benefiting the private sector. This resulted in small and medium hospitals seeking empanelment as a means to ensure regular patient supply. The public insurance scheme is an avenue for attracting patients, and in several districts, these hospitals withdraw from the scheme after getting considerable amount of money and patient load. Thus, the scheme is misusing the insurance scheme in order to serve private interests. The condition of several other hospitals was also quite similar, some were considering de-empanelling themselves and some face de-empanelment as a result of fraudulent acts.

The fact that most of the private hospitals empanel to attract patients and later de-empanel themselves should raise an alarm with the authorities who are involved in the administration of such schemes and also look into aspects of fraud, wrong doing and also diversion of funds.

The developments on the political front have meant that the scheme must undergo changes according to the whims of the new government. The comprehensiveness has already been compromised with; now the inclusiveness and coverage has been made optional. From the viewpoint of the current card holders, the future is uncertain; being a centrally sponsored scheme it might continue to exist, but when there are parallel schemes being brought out by the government, fate of the old one hangs in balance. The scheme had been running for more than 2 years, and continues to generate headlines for its wide coverage and adaptation in even far off countries (Minivan News, 2011), is being looked down upon in one of the states where it has been running successfully ever since its launch (Nayar, 2010).

The analysis of the scheme and its working would be incomplete without the discussion about the process of empanelment, the ways in which some single doctor dispensaries were empanelled and the way in which the conditionality for empanelment were disregarded. The dilution of norms during empanelment was overlooked; this had led to some hospitals making it to the empanelled list and functioning for a long time. Some hospitals were found to have no qualified doctors; at some places, the doctors were roped in for the period of inspection and were sent off after the hospital got its accreditation. These incidents point to the absence of any strict checks before empanelment.

The future of the scheme depends on political will of the government, as well as the capacity in understanding the need and effectiveness of such a scheme. Until that is achieved, the scheme may be scuttled and its working tampered with. The introduction of new schemes is not the answer to the inequalities that exist; the ones that were started must be run effectively to notice a change in the conditions. In the current scenario, every year during the budget session, new promises are made and new schemes announced; by the time they materialise, it is time for another election and change in policies and programmes. Until the administration decides to stick with one scheme and its working, it is difficult to gauge the impact it made and the necessary changes to be brought about to make it more effective.

The scheme has changed in the way it works; post the original data collection time period, there have been changes in the number of hospitals that are empanelled; some have continued to stay in the race of empanelment and some have lost out. The most noticeable feature that has undergone change is the distinction that the scheme is no longer available for the APL population, the cards that were once issued, some have fallen out of use and some could not be renewed. Only very few remain in use. One of the more positive changes that have come about after the new government took charge was the inclusion of 57 new categories of beneficiaries. These include coir workers, street vendors, as well as all families whose family income is less than ₹600 per month.

The number of hospitals that are currently empanelled stands at 26, and is equally distributed in 13 private hospitals and 13 public hospitals. Some of these hospitals include ones that had de-empanelled themselves and have managed to re-empanel in the years after the initial study and data collection was done.

References

Anon (2011). "The State of India's Welfare State: Ropey Nets", *The Economist*. May 18. Available at: *http://www.economist.com/blogs/freeexchange/2011/05/state_indias_welfare_state* (accessed 20 May 2011).

Borowitz, M. and R. Atun (2006). "The Unfinished Journey from Semashko to Bismarck: Health Reform in Central Asia from 1991 to 2006", *Central Asian Survey* 25(4): 419-40.

Baru, R. (2006). "Financing Health Service: Alternative to Private Insurance", in S. Prasad and C. Sathyamala (eds.) (2006), *Securing Health for All*. New Delhi: Institute of Human Development.

Criel, Bart, Kent Ranson, N. Devadasan and Wim Van Damme (2004). "Community Health Insurance in India: An Overview", *Economic and Political Weekly* XXXIX(28): 3170-83, July 10.

Dror, D. (2006). "Health Insurance for the Poor: Myths and Realities", *Economic and Political Weekly* 4541-44, 4 November.

Escobar, Maria-Luisa, Charles C. Griffin and R. Paul Shaw (2011). *The Impact of Health Insurance in Low and Middle Income Countries*. Washington DC: Brookings Institution Press. p.xi.

Harlankar, S. (2010). "The Master Card", *Hindustan Times*, July 04. Available at: *http://www.hindustantimes.com/StoryPage/Print/567469.aspx* (accessed on 23 July 2011).

Krishnakumar, R. (2008). "Healthy Scheme", *The Hindu*. Available at: *http://www.hindu.com/fline/fl2522/stories/20081107252203300.htm* (accessed on 19 May 2011).

Maya, C. (2010). "Medical College Hospitals Bogged Down by RSBY", *The Hindu*, p.03.

Minivan News (2011). "News Report Links Maldives to Indian Health Insurance Scheme", *Minivan News*, July 03. Available at: *http://minivannews.com/news-in-brief/news-report-links-maldives-to-indian-health-insurance-scheme-22113* (accessed on 3 July 2011).

Nair, C.G. (2008). "Health Insurance for One Crore People", *The Hindu*. p.1.

Nayar, L. (2010). "The Card Reads You", *Outlook*. March 22. Available at: *http://www.outlookindia.com/article.aspx?264636* (accessed on 19 May 2011)

Rai, Sheila and Niha Rai (2010). "Rashtriya Swasthya Bima Yojana (RSBY): Panacea for the Poor". Available at *http//:www.napsipag.org/SHEILA%20RAI%20&%20NIHA%20RAI.pdf* (accessed on 5 May 2011).

Rajalakshmi, T.K. (2011). "Vague Promise", *Frontline* 28(15), July 16-29. Available at: *http://www.frontline.in/stories/20110729281509700.htm* (accessed on 12 July 2011).

Rajasekhar, D., Erlend Berg, Maitreesh Ghatak, R. Manjula, Sanchari Roy (2011). "Implementing Health Insurance for the Poor: The Rollout of RSBY in Karnataka", Economic Organisation and Public Policy Programme Series EOPP/2011/25. March. London: The Suntory Centre, Suntory and Toyota International Centres for Economics and Related Disciplines, London School of Economics and Political Science.

Rajiv, G. (2008). "Doctors Open a "no-frill" Hospital", *Indian Express*. Available at *http://www.newindianexpress.com/states/kerala/article19912.ece* (accessed on 26 June 2011).

Sen, Amartya (2011). "Gigantic Inequalities in Access to Healthcare", *The Hindu*. July 10. Available at: *http://www.thehindu.com/news/national/article2215872.ece?homepage=true* (accessed on 10 July 2011).

Shiva Kumar, A.K., Arnab Acharya, K. Nagaraj, Rama Baru and Sanghmitra Acharya (2010). "Inequities in Access to Health Services in India: Caste, Class and Religion", *Economic and Political Weekly* XLV(38): 49-58, 18 September.

Swarup, A. (2011). "RSBY Emerging Scenario", Avalable at: *http://www.rsby.gov.in/Documents.aspx* (accessed on May 2011).

Websites

Eleventh Five year Plan Document. (accessed on 11 June 2011).

Government of Kerala, G.O No.17571/J2/07/LBR.

Government of Kerala, G.O(P)No. 95/2008/LBR dated 4 July 2008, Labour and Rehabilitation (J) Department.

"Health Insurance in India: Current Scenario", *http://www.searo.who.int/linkfiles/social_health_insurance_an2.pdf* (accessed on 3 May 2011).